a heart that dances

a heart that dances

SATISFY YOUR DESIRE FOR INTIMACY WITH GOD

Come with me by yourselves
to a quiet place . . .
JESUS IN MARK 6:31 (NIV)

catherine martin

NAVPRESS

Bringing Truth to Life
P.O. Box 35001, Colorado Springs, Colorado 80935

OUR GUARANTEE TO YOU

We believe so strongly in the message of our books that we are making this quality guarantee to you. If for any reason you are disappointed with the content of this book, return the title page to us with your name and address and we will refund to you the list price of the book. To help us serve you better, please briefly describe why you were disappointed. Mail your refund request to: NavPress, P.O. Box 35002, Colorado Springs, CO 80935.

The Navigators is an international Christian organization. Our mission is to reach, disciple, and equip people to know Christ and to make Him known through successive generations. We envision multitudes of diverse people in the United States and every other nation who have a passionate love for Christ, live a lifestyle of sharing Christ's love, and multiply spiritual laborers among those without Christ.

NavPress is the publishing ministry of The Navigators. NavPress publications help believers learn biblical truth and apply what they learn to their lives and ministries. Our mission is to stimulate spiritual formation among our readers.

Cover design by David Carlson Design
Cover image by Albert Normandin/Masterfile
Creative Team: Terry Behimer, Karen Lee-Thorp, Pat Miller

Some of the anecdotal illustrations in this book are true to life and are included with the permission of the persons involved. All other illustrations are composites of real situations, and any resemblance to people living or dead is coincidental.

Printed in the United States of America

1 2 3 4 5 6 7 8 9 10 / 07 06 05 04 03

FOR A FREE CATALOG OF
NAVPRESS BOOKS & BIBLE STUDIES,
CALL 1-800-366-7788 (USA)
OR 1-416-499-4615 (CANADA)

contents

foreword

I was so young that I can't recall exactly when I started reading the Bible every day. My parents taught me to read God's Word daily, and my dad's example of opening the Bible each morning was an ongoing testimony of the importance of personal Scripture intake. All the Sunday school teachers during my childhood asked each child present at the beginning of class: "Did you read your Bible every day this week?" So I grew up in a spiritual climate where looking to God through His Word on a regular basis was both modeled and expected.

The Lord showed me my need for Christ and granted me repentance and faith in Him when I was nine. That's when the Holy Spirit caused my heart to begin "crying, 'Abba! Father!'" (Galatians 4:6), and my prayer life as a believer was born. After each day's Bible reading, I usually uttered a brief, simple prayer to the Lord.

Since my first days as a Christian, my spiritual progress has almost always been in direct proportion to the growth of my daily quiet time. And there have been many helps and turning points along the way. One of the first was a book on prayer—the first Christian book I ever read—that affected my prayer life during my college days. Sermons, conferences, Bible studies, testimonies, conversations, books, prayer meetings—all have been tools in the Lord's hands to shape and turn my devotional experience with Him.

Among them were two interactive books I used during and shortly after my seminary years. One of them guided me through my daily time in the Word and the other in prayer. I look back on my many hours with these volumes as among the sweetest and most formative devotional experiences of my life.

I'm confident that in the years to come, many will say the same kinds of things about their encounters with the Lord that were prompted by Catherine Martin's *A Heart That Dances*.

DONALD S. WHITNEY
www.SpiritualDisciplines.org

acknowledgments

Thank you to my husband, David Martin, M.D., for encouraging me to give my utmost for His highest. You always help me give my best, and you always love me with an unconditional love.

Thank you to the best family in the world. Mother, you taught me how to express my heart in writing and gave me such a love for reading and books. Dad, you make me laugh and encourage me to go for it in life. Rob, Tania, Chris, and Kayla—what a joy you are to me. Rob, I love your phone calls at six in the morning to tell me what new thing our little Kayla has done. Eloise, thank you for the surprises you give me. You have kept me going many times! Andy, Ann, Keegan, and James, I love you. Nana, I love you.

And now for those of you who are my dear friends: Andy Kotner, thank you for doing all my quiet times at your own pace and for phoning me to ask what I meant by certain questions. It has been a great thing to share life—both the joys and the sorrows—with you. Conni Hudson, you have been such a heart friend for me—thank you for loving the Lord and me. I love our breakfasts together. Thank you for leading the pilot of *A Heart That Dances*. You are a teacher *par excellence!* Cindy Clark, thank you for your great and abiding encouragement. You have been a steadfast friend who has helped me to dare to dream God's dreams and then actually see Him bring them about. Thank you, Beverly Trupp, for believing in me and for being such an example for me. Thank you for being a sounding board as I talk with you about my hopes and dreams. Thank you, Kelly Abeyratne, for praying with me and for being present to share my thoughts and ideas. Thank you, Myra Murphy, for carrying out the dream of our Revive My Heart O Lord Women's Revival Gatherings. Who knows what the Lord is going to do in the days to come? Thank you to all those who piloted *A Heart That Dances:* Janet Teurle, Karen Mounce, Cindy Clark, Sharon Hastings, Linda Nichols, Shawna Koon, Conni Hudson, Bev Trupp, Connie Sparks, Joanna Akers, Jane Jeffers, Kayla Branscum, Sue Meyers, Dawn Ivie, and Julie Brauchmann.

A very special thank you to Kayla Branscum, my assistant at Quiet Time Ministries. Kayla, we could never have done everything that we did in the last year without your diligence and organization. Thank you for using your gifts to serve the Lord. Thank you as always to Josh and Dottie McDowell and the Josh McDowell Ministry for being a source of encouragement and inspiration to me. Also, a big thank you to Vonette Bright for calling me at a very opportune time in the writing of this book. Your call was such an encouragement to me! And then, thank you to the women at Southwest Community Church in Indian Wells, California. I love ministering together with you. Thank you for being those radical disciples who have a reckless abandonment to the Lord. Thank you, Karen Mounce, for helping me to serve the Lord at SCC. Thank you, Stefanie Kelly, for meeting with me weekly to share in my adventure of writing these quiet times. Thank you to the pastors and staff at Southwest Community Church, especially pastors Dave Moore and Ron Baum for your support and encouragement.

Thank you to Jack Smith, publisher at Banner Of Truth, for noticing these books of quiet times and recommending them to NavPress. Talking with you that day on the phone was a defining moment for me. And thank you, Kent Wilson, publisher at NavPress, as well as Terry Behimer and Toben Heim, for sharing my passion to see the truth of God's Word become a reality in others' lives. It is a total joy to work with you. Thank you to Amy Spencer for your great attention to detail and your gracious help in the publishing of this book. Thank you, Karen Lee-Thorp, for your brilliance in editing. Thank you to Curtis Yates and Sealy Yates for encouraging me to do what God has called me to do. Thank you to Luci Swindoll for a very special phone call offering words of wisdom that I will never forget. Thank you to Marilyn Meberg for encouraging me in ministry. A special thanks to Mr. Paul DeVries, senior publisher of Discovery House Publishers, and Sonya Williams, permissions editor at Discovery House, for your wisdom in prompting me to listen to the Lord about my title: *A Heart That Dances.* I learned something important in following the Lord's lead, and that's what intimacy is all about.

Thank you to the Quiet Time Ministries Dream Team, who partner with me in this ministry that God is using worldwide to teach devotion to God and His Word. This book would never have made it to press without you. A special thanks to Connie and Grady Sparks and Cindy and Drew Clark for encouraging the vision and dream of Quiet Time Ministries. Thank you to so many who volunteer time and energy to work together with me in the trenches, including Pat Pearce, Joan Krause, and Barbara Wohlford. Thank you to the board of directors of Quiet Time Ministries for being such great advisors: Conni Hudson, Shirley Peters, Jane Lyons, and my husband. Thank you to the *Enriching Your Quiet Time* magazine staff: Shirley Peters, Cay Hough, Maurine Cromwell, Laurie Bailey, and Conni Hudson. You have explored these truths with me about intimacy with God.

intimacy with God

There's a mountain in Sedona, Arizona, that offers the best view of one of the most beautiful canyons in the world. It takes at least an hour to get to the top, but the journey is worth the climb. From the top of this mountain, you can see for miles.

I have always loved mountains. There's something about their majesty, what grows on them, the surprises as one climbs, and the view at the top. Each step of the journey up a mountain involves change: a change in view, in incline, in altitude, and in the stride and pace of the one climbing. There are bends in the road, and if you fail to turn, the journey stops. When you finally adapt to the new level and continue to climb, the adventure begins again.

The most majestic and rewarding mountain of all is the mountain of God Himself. You and I are invited to engage in an amazing adventure: *the adventure of knowing God.* God says, "Be still, and know that I am God" (Psalm 46:10, NIV). He invites you to engage in something with Him that is much deeper than surface acquaintance. That word *know* implies familiarity, depth, and the kind of intimacy usually reserved for marriage. Intimacy is a relationship that goes deep and is marked by friendship and emotional closeness. It is private and personal. There is love, warmth, and intense joy in intimacy. And it takes time. It grows through experience and engagement with another. This intimacy is what God desires with you.

When I first entered into a relationship with the Lord thirty years ago, I had no idea of the depth of intimacy God desired to have with me. I thought of knowing God as a religion, a way of life. However, I discovered that this way of life must be lived in the context of an ever-deepening relationship with God Himself. The way of life grows out of the relationship.

If you pursue the life without pursuing God, you will eventually burn out and stop the journey. However, if you have truly invited Christ into your life, then God will not leave you at the side of the road. He will come alongside you and bid you to rise up and continue on with Him. "Come dance with Me," He calls. It is not just a walk, but a dance of the heart as you keep in step with the Lord. He invites you to dance with Him, go to new places, and gaze upon dimensions of His character that you have yet to experience. He wants to reveal the secrets of His ways and purposes. "No eye has seen, no ear has heard, no mind has conceived what God has prepared for those who love him" (1 Corinthians 2:9, NIV).

This invitation to dance in your heart with Him resonates throughout Scripture.

- "Be still, and know that I am God" (Psalm 46:10, NIV).
- King David danced "before the LORD with all his might" (2 Samuel 6:14). His firm resolve was, "I will celebrate before the LORD" (2 Samuel 6:21).

- "Let him who boasts boast about this, that he understands and knows Me, that I am the LORD" (Jeremiah 9:24).
- "You will seek me and find me when you seek me with all your heart" (Jeremiah 29:13, NIV).
- "I am now going to allure her; I will lead her into the desert and speak tenderly to her" (Hosea 2:14, NIV).
- "Draw near to God and He will draw near to you" (James 4:8).
- "Come with me by yourselves to a quiet place and get some rest" (Mark 6:31, NIV).
- "Here I am! I stand at the door and knock. If anyone hears my voice and opens the door, I will come in and eat with him, and he with me" (Revelation 3:20, NIV).

I got excited when I discovered that God desired an intimate relationship with me. I set aside the playthings of the world and engaged in the adventure, the great dance of the heart with the Lord.

A number of books were instrumental in my journey. In *The Pursuit of God* by A. W. Tozer, I learned how holy men and women of the past "want[ed] to taste, to touch with their hearts, to see with their inner eyes the wonder that is God."[1] That statement changed how I approached the Word of God. Now I was on a quest to discover how each man or woman in the Bible engaged in his or her relationship with God. God began to show me secrets about the pursuit to know Him. (I say "secrets" because they are not manifestly evident to the casual onlooker who isn't willing to tarry in one place in God's Word.) I saw how David, the man after God's own heart, had an intense desire for God even as a young boy. I saw how knowing the Lord changed Jacob. I observed how Noah walked with God and stood out in his generation. I looked at the people of Israel, God's chosen people, and noticed how they walked away from their relationship with God. As I learned, I began to climb higher up the great and awesome mountain of God.

Knowing God by J. I. Packer taught me to go beyond lazily reading words to engaging in deep thought about truth. I began to try to wrap my mind around different aspects of God's character. Even though I could never plumb the depths of His character, I could at least attempt to articulate my understanding of the truth. I began to write my thoughts in a journal. In my feeble attempts at articulation came a new understanding and experience of His person and character. I began to dialogue with God with a new understanding of who He was. It humbled me to walk and talk with Him and then actually begin to dance with Him, knowing how majestic He was. I began to obey Him in new ways because I had an ever-increasing reverence for Him. I decided that if knowing God was what life was all about, and if He revealed Himself in His Word, then the greatest thing I could do was give myself to living in the Bible, His Word.

My Utmost for His Highest by Oswald Chambers taught me to become a radical disciple of Jesus Christ. Chambers encouraged me to know that there is nothing else, no other pursuit, that even remotely compares to the pursuit of God.

I remember meeting with an older Dutch woman named Thea, who had introduced me to the writings of A. W. Tozer. We would meet in her home and study the book of Romans.

The first thing we would do is pray. Sometimes Thea would break into a quiet sob before saying anything, because she was so overwhelmed by the majesty of God. I saw in living color what it meant to be on this pursuit of God. When I think of Thea, I think of Jesus Christ. She is now with the Lord, but she will always be that living example of someone who knew God.

The Word of God has been my greatest influence in unlocking the door to intimacy with God. There is so much treasure contained in the Bible that I cannot recommend it highly enough. One of the most important things you can do is to choose a Bible translation that is meaningful to you and then live in it, making it your own. You can never spend too much time in God's Word. Get to know it so well that not only have you made your home in it, but it also has made its home in your heart.

God has given me a rich and full life. The substance of this life has been the great adventure of knowing God. In the triumph and the tragedy that has taken place in my own life, God's presence has been the deep, life-giving water. No matter where I am, no matter what I am doing, He is there. And He is everything I need. As Tozer said, there is no limit to the dimensions of God's character or the depth of His Word. The treasure is there for the taking, if only we will go with God.

A Heart That Dances will take you on the great adventure of intimacy with God. I want you to experience firsthand the joy of life with the Lord as the celebration it truly is. To this end, you'll look at how various biblical characters interacted with God. You will discover David, the man after God's own heart, and Moses, the one who spoke face to face with God as a man speaks with a friend. You will look at the people of Israel to learn about God's heart of love for them. You will reflect on the special relationship the Old Testament prophets had with their Lord. And you will learn from His followers in the New Testament.

The quiet times are organized according to the plan that was developed and is taught by Quiet Time Ministries: P.R.A.Y.E.R.™[2] Each day this plan includes:

Prepare your heart
Read and study God's Word
Adore God in prayer
Yield yourself to God
Enjoy His presence
Rest in His love

Your quiet times will include devotional readings, devotional Bible study, journaling, prayer, worship, meditating on hymns, and application of God's Word in your life. In the back of this book, you will find Journal Pages and Prayer Pages for you to record your thoughts and prayer requests. With this book and your Bible, you have everything you need for quiet time with the Lord.

These quiet times will encourage you to be a participant instead of an observer. That is what quiet time with God is all about. I trust that you will experience rich times alone with

God. Set aside a time and place to be with Him. Organize all your materials in one place.

For help in learning more about quiet time, I encourage you to read my book, *Radical Intimacy—How to Really Have a Quiet Time*, published by Quiet Time Ministries. You may also wish to visit Quiet Time Ministries Online at www.quiettime.org for more encouragement. *A Heart That Dances* is designed to help you become consistent in quiet time so that you might know God and love Him more. If you would like to lead a group through *A Heart That Dances*, a leader's guide with discussion questions is available from Quiet Time Ministries, as are accompanying messages on videotape and audiotape.

God is saying to you, "Will you dance with Me?" Will you come away with Him, engage in the great adventure, and celebrate before the Lord? If so, then you are in for the time of your life. There will be hills and valleys, but the view is breathtaking. As the psalmist said, "Taste and see that the LORD is good. Oh, the joys of those who trust in him!" (Psalm 34:8, NLT).

The Road of Life

At first I saw God as my observer, my judge,
keeping track of the things I did wrong,
so as to know whether I merited heaven
or hell when I die.
He was out there sort of like a president.
I recognized His picture when I saw it,
but I really didn't know Him.
But later on when I met Christ,
it seemed as though life were rather like a bike ride,
but it was a tandem bike,
and I noticed that Christ
was in the back helping me pedal.
I don't know just when it was
that He suggested we change places,
but life has not been the same since.
When I had control,
I knew the way.
It was rather boring,
but predictable. . . .
It was the shortest distance between two points.
But when He took the lead,
He knew delightful long cuts,
up mountains,
and through rocky places

at breakneck speeds.
It was all I could do to hang on!
Even though it looked like madness,
He said, *Pedal!*
I worried and was anxious and asked,
Where are you taking me?
He laughed and didn't answer,
and I started to learn to trust.
I forgot my boring life
and entered into the adventure.
And when I'd say, *I'm scared,*
He'd lean back and touch my hand.
He took me to people with gifts that I needed,
gifts of healing,
acceptance
and joy.
They gave me gifts to take on my journey,
my Lord's and mine.
And we were off again.
He said, *Give the gifts away;*
they're extra baggage, too much weight.
So I did,
to the people we met,
and I found that in giving I received,
and still our burden was light.
I did not trust Him,
at first,
in control of my life.
I thought He'd wreck it;
but He knows bike secrets,
knows how to make it bend to take sharp corners,
knows how to jump to clear high rocks,
knows how to fly to shorten scary passages.
And I am learning to be quiet
and pedal in the strangest places,
and I'm beginning to enjoy the view
and the cool breeze on my face
with my delightful constant companion, Jesus Christ.
And when I'm sure I just can't do any more,
He just smiles and says . . . *Pedal.*

AUTHOR UNKNOWN

LETTER TO THE LORD

Where are you in this dance of the heart with God? How is your relationship with Him? Have you been spending time with Him on a consistent basis? Take a few moments to write a prayer to the Lord in the form of a letter, asking Him to speak to you during your time in *A Heart That Dances*. Ask Him to change your life as you spend time with Him in His Word.

the invitation to intimacy

week
one

PSALM 46:10

personal relationship

Be . . .
PSALM 46:10, NIV

Prepare Your Heart

Has anyone ever remarked about how religious you are? Many people think that if you talk about God or go to church a lot, then you must be religious. But if you read the Bible for very long, you'll find that people are really into religion, but God is really into relationships. People tend to want to *do*, but God emphasizes above all that His people should simply *be*. He wants them to *be* with Him, to *be* the unique persons that He made them to *be*. This week you will study intimacy with God. This study is about *relationship*. The most important relationship you will ever have is your relationship with God. Do you know God? Are you in a relationship with Him?

Two thousand years ago an amazing Person lived in the area of Jerusalem. This man's name was Jesus. He did amazing miracles. And basically, He astounded all who came into contact with Him. And He made an amazing claim—He claimed to be God!

The religious leaders of the day were waiting for a Messiah, a man from God, but they expected Him to come as a king who would align himself with them and give them power. These religious leaders were offended by Jesus because He seemed to enjoy associating with people of ill repute, people who were poor, people they considered sinners. But it was His claim to being God and His offer of forgiveness of sins and the gift of eternal life that blew them away. And it was this very claim that also drew masses of people to Him to hear what He had to say. As people came to hear His words, Jesus did amazing things.

He would touch someone who was paralyzed, and that person would walk. He would speak to a prostitute, and as tears came to her eyes, she would be filled with the desire to be holy and righteous and good. He would place His hands on the eyes of one who had been blind from birth, and for the first time, that person would have sight. And after three years, people from virtually the entire area of Judea and Galilee flocked to be with Jesus.

The religious leaders plotted to kill Jesus, not because of what He did, but because of Who He claimed to be—God in the flesh. One well-known columnist was asked who he would most like to have interviewed from across history. He named Jesus Christ. He said he would like to ask Jesus if He was indeed born of a virgin, because he felt that the answer to that question would define history.

Could it be that God has visited us on earth—that Jesus is God? Why would Jesus come to earth?

Suppose there is a God who is Creator—One who created the heavens, the earth, and you and me. Suppose He created human beings, including you, for a purpose. And that purpose was simple: He wanted a love relationship with them—and with you. Suppose that relationship existed in the beginning. Suppose when God created the first human beings, the relationship was idyllic, and the fellowship and the exchange of love between God and His creation were perfect. Within that idyllic existence, God Himself set up boundaries to allow for this love relationship to flourish. The boundaries were basic: God's creation was not to exist independently of Him but was to be dependent upon Him as the source of everything.

Then one day God's human beings crossed those boundaries. Suppose they decided, with the help of one who was bent on destroying their relationship with God, to make a choice that was independent and directly against what God had commanded. Once they crossed that boundary, sin entered the world.

Now suppose that when sin entered the world, the love relationship with God was affected: their sin separated them from a holy God, and they could no longer enjoy this intimate fellowship with Him for which they were designed. This sin created a great uncrossable chasm between man and God and affected all of mankind.

The Bible tells us that "all have sinned and fall short of the glory of God" (Romans 3:23) and that the sentence, or penalty, for sin is death (see Romans 6:23).

Now let us suppose that God saw the inability of man to reach Him because of sin. Because He knew it was impossible for man to reach Him, He reached down to man and determined to pay the penalty for sin Himself.

It is a fact of history that the Jewish leaders arrested Jesus at night, secretly tried Him, and pressured the Roman governor to execute him. While Jesus was on the cross, His followers mourned. His disciples had fled, fearing for their own lives. His death devastated those who knew and loved Him. Three days later, something happened—something Jesus had said would happen: He rose from the dead. He appeared to His disciples and more than five hundred others.

Jesus is who He claimed to be: God has spoken in Jesus.

Only God has a love for you that is greater than any found in this world. What does He desire from you more than anything else? Your love. You are what gives Him the greatest pleasure. Augustine wrote, "You have made us for Yourself, Oh God, and our hearts are restless until they find their rest in You."[1] Perhaps you are thinking, Yes, this is exactly what I am longing for. I would like to know God. How can you have a relationship with Him?

God is offering you the gift of a relationship through Jesus Christ. This gift does not become yours until you actually receive it. To establish your relationship with God, simply turn to Him, ask Him to forgive your sins, and invite Christ into your life. The Bible teaches that "as many as received [Christ], to them He gave the right to become children of God, even to those who believe in His name" (John 1:12).

If your heart is restless and you long to know God, you may pray a simple prayer to invite Him into your heart. If you have never asked Him into your life, you may pray the following: *Lord Jesus, I need You. Thank You for dying on the cross for me. I ask You now to come into my life, forgive my sins, and make me the person You want me to be. In Jesus' name, Amen.*

READ AND STUDY GOD'S WORD

This week you are going to look at God's invitation to an intimate relationship. In Psalm 46:10, God says, "Be still, and know that I am God." What do those words mean? As we delve more deeply into this great invitation, it is important to stop and think about where you are in your relationship with God. What has God been doing in your life in the last six months? What has He been teaching you? Is there a verse or passage of Scripture that has been particularly significant to you during the past year? Record your thoughts below or on a Journal Page in the back of this book.

1. Read Psalm 46. What is most significant in this psalm to you today?

God is powerful & we should listen to him

2. Write Psalm 46:10, word for word. What is your favorite part of that verse and why?

Be silent & know that I am God I will be honored by every nation I will be honored throughout the world God is powerful be still & listen to him.

3. God's invitation to a personal relationship is found throughout Scripture. Look at the following verses and record what you learn about God's invitation.

2 Chronicles 7:14

Jeremiah 9:23-24

Zechariah 1:1-3

Matthew 11:28-29

James 4:8

Revelation 3:20

Summarize what you have seen about God's invitation to you.

He is always here for us all we have to do is ask

ADORE GOD IN PRAYER

At the outset of this study, as you think about intimacy with God, take some time now to write a prayer to God below or in the Journal Pages. Include in this prayer your desire to know God more. Ask God to speak to you as you draw near to Him.

YIELD YOURSELF TO GOD

As you think about God's invitation to a personal relationship, meditate on these words by John Piper in his book *Desiring God*:

> The faith which pleases God is the assurance that when we turn to him we will find that All-satisfying Treasure. We will find our heart's eternal delight. . . . Once we had no delight in God, and Christ was just a vague historical figure. What we enjoyed was food and friendships and productivity and investments and vacations and hobbies and games and reading and shopping and sex and sports and art and TV and travel . . . but not God. He was an idea—even a good one—and a topic for discussion; but he was not a treasure of delight. Then something miraculous happened. It was like the opening of the eyes of the blind during the golden dawn. First the stunned silence before the unspeakable beauty of holiness. Then a shock and terror that we had actually loved the darkness. Then the settling stillness of joy that this is the soul's end. The quest is over. We would give anything if we might be granted to live in the presence of this glory forever and ever. And then, faith—the confidence that Christ has made a way for me, a sinner, to live in his glorious fellowship forever, the confidence that if I come to God through Christ, he will give me the desire of my heart to share his holiness and behold his glory.[2]

ENJOY HIS PRESENCE

How would you describe your relationship with the Lord? Is it personal and intimate? Have you responded to God's invitation? What would you like to see happen in your relationship with Him? Record your thoughts.

REST IN HIS LOVE

"Here I am! I stand at the door and knock. If anyone hears my voice and opens the door, I will come in and eat with him, and he with me" (Revelation 3:20, NIV).

quiet rest

Be still . . .
PSALM 46:10, NIV

Prepare Your Heart

Silence and solitude are the great secrets to knowing God intimately. They are almost lost arts in the twenty-first century. Have you learned to *be still*? This phrase means to stop, let go, and relax. The Lord is inviting you to this stillness. Why? Because He wants to reveal Himself to you. As you begin your quiet time today, ask the Lord to quiet your heart and speak to you. You may wish to write a simple prayer to the Lord.

READ AND STUDY GOD'S WORD

When God says, "Be still," He is asking you to stop, relax, and know that He is God. The Hebrew word means "to relax the hands" and "let down." In a world that is moving faster and faster, we need to stop and turn from busyness to be still. God teaches His people this stillness throughout the Bible. Jesus demonstrated it with His life.

1. Turn to Luke 5:15-16. What do you notice about Jesus' life and habits?

that he stopped & took time for himself & to pray

2. Think about the following verses and record your insights related to silence and solitude.

1 Kings 19:9-13

Psalm 131

Isaiah 30:15

Isaiah 32:17-18

Micah 6:8

Zephaniah 3:17

1 Timothy 2:1-4

3. What is the value of silence and solitude in becoming intimate with God?

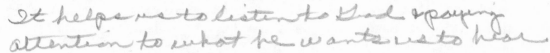

It helps us to listen to God + paying attention to what he wants us to hear

ADORE GOD IN PRAYER

Take some time now to be still before the Lord. What are those things that are weighing heavily on your heart today? If anything is troubling your soul, turn to the Prayer Pages in the back of this book and write out each one as a prayer request, laying everything at the throne of God.

YIELD YOURSELF TO GOD

When we come to Him in prayer, we should begin as one who has come to the highest place a soul may reach—to God Himself. We must see ourselves as standing at the wellspring of overflowing goodness! It is so honoring to God to come to Him in prayer, declaring His goodness over all. And it brings so much sweetness to the soul. So many miss this, and it is the *true beginning of prayer.* Come to Him, then, and start your prayers by resting quietly and completely in His goodness. You will quickly find this inner rest is the very thing that makes it possible for Him to flood us with the power of grace—pouring himself into us . . . and out to others through us.[1]

JULIAN OF NORWICH IN *I PROMISE YOU A CROWN*

ENJOY HIS PRESENCE

As you launch out on the great adventure of knowing God, your daily quiet time will be the most important part of your day. How can you become consistent? The best way is to set aside a time and a place to be alone with God.

When life is so busy, it is not always easy to find time. Consequently, you must resolve to be intentional, carving time out of your day so that you can be alone with God and listen to what He has to say to you. If the CEO of your company or the president of the United States called you up and asked you to lunch, would you write it on your calendar? Then, would you show up? Spending time with God is even more vital than spending time with the president of the United States. After all, He is the CEO of the universe!

Find a quiet place to be alone with the Lord. Organize all your quiet time materials in that place. You might use a basket or a shelf to keep the materials together.

Once you have found a time and a place, then you need a plan to spend time with the Lord. That is one of the purposes of this book. It gives you a plan that you will learn over the course of the study. This plan—P.R.A.Y.E.R.™—offers many exciting ways to draw near to God in quiet time. When you draw near to God, He will draw near to you (see James 4:8).

As you close your time with the Lord today, think about what it means to be still. What elements of your time with God will help you to be still so that you may know God more? Is anything in your life keeping you from being still as you approach God and spend time with Him? Write your thoughts below or in the Journal Pages.

Rest in His Love

"Are you tired? Worn out? Burned out on religion? Come to me. Get away with me and you'll recover your life. I'll show you how to take a real rest. Walk with me and work with me— watch how I do it. Learn the unforced rhythms of grace. I won't lay anything heavy or ill-fitting on you. Keep company with me and you'll learn to live freely and lightly" (Matthew 11:28-29, MSG).

intimate experience

Be still, and know . . .
PSALM 46:10, NIV

Prepare Your Heart

Nicholas Herman was a soldier in the Thirty Years War that engulfed seventeenth-century Europe. At the age of eighteen he was captured, charged with espionage, and threatened with hanging. He proclaimed his innocence and was released. Shortly after, he was wounded and left the army. What he witnessed in the war led him to give his life to Christ that same year. He briefly served the treasurer of the king of France, but soon he decided to dedicate himself to God and become a monk. At a Carmelite monastery, he was given the name Brother Lawrence and became a full member of the order in 1642.

His assigned duties at the monastery were in the kitchen. He hated his job for at least ten years. One day he made a conscious decision to live in the presence of God, moment by moment, walking and talking with Him throughout the day. He described the result of that decision: "I suddenly found myself changed, and my soul, which up till then was always disturbed, experienced a profound interior peace." He no longer dreaded his kitchen work, and he felt close to God whether he was peeling potatoes or kneeling at the altar. His inner peace was so profound that others were drawn to him. His reputation for holiness led to the publication of a collection of his letters and reminiscences, which was later published as *The Practice of the Presence of God*.

Brother Lawrence drew near to God in his everyday experience. In doing so, he developed an intimate relationship with God. When God invites us to *know*, what does He mean? The Hebrew word translated "to know" (*yada*) means to understand personally by experience. It means intimacy. God wants us to understand His character, to be intimately acquainted with all His ways. Only as we take what we learn from His Word and then live it out, moment by moment with the Lord, will we experience Him as He works in and through us.

Today you are going to have the opportunity to draw near to the Lord and think about what it means to know Him. As you begin this time, turn to Psalm 42. Meditate on these words and record the phrase that is most significant to you today. Ask God to quiet your heart and speak to you.

2- I thirst for God the living God- when can I come + stand before him?

READ AND STUDY GOD'S WORD

Throughout Scripture, God asks His people to *know* Him. We cannot know anything beyond what He chooses to reveal. The glorious truth is that He has revealed much about Himself to many different men and women. He has revealed Himself in His creation, in Jesus, and in His Word.

　　1. Read the following passages. In what way did each person come to know God?
　　　　Genesis 21:9-21 (Hagar)

　　　　1 Samuel 3 (the boy Samuel)

　　　　John 8:1-11 (the woman caught in adultery)

　　2. Look at the following verses and record what you learn about knowing God. Include in your insights what you see about God's heart. If you are short on time, you might choose two of the passages and come back to the others at another time.
　　　　Exodus 29:44-46

　　　　Deuteronomy 4:30-40

　　　　Deuteronomy 7:9

1 Samuel 2:12

Psalm 9:10

Psalm 36:9-10

Psalm 95:8-11

Jeremiah 31:33-34

Daniel 11:32

Hosea 2:19-20

Hosea 6:3

John 17:3

Ephesians 3:19

Philippians 3:8-11

3. What have you learned about knowing God?

ADORE GOD IN PRAYER

Lord, teach me to listen. The times are noisy and my ears are weary with the thousand raucous sounds which continuously assault them. Give me the spirit of the boy Samuel when he said to Thee, *speak, for Thy servant heareth.* Let me hear Thee speaking in my heart. Let me get used to the sound of Thy voice, that its tones may be familiar when the sounds of earth die away and the only sound will be the music of Thy speaking voice. Amen.[1]

A. W. TOZER IN *THE PURSUIT OF GOD*

YIELD YOURSELF TO GOD

The world is perishing for lack of the knowledge of God, and the church is famishing for want of His presence. The instant cure of most of our religious ills would be to enter the Presence in spiritual experience, to become suddenly aware that we are in God and God is in us. This would lift us out of our pitiful narrowness and cause our hearts to be enlarged. This would burn away the impurities from our lives as the bugs and fungi were burned away by the fire that dwelt in the bush. What a broad world to roam in, what a sea to swim in is this God and Father of our Lord Jesus Christ.[2]

A. W. TOZER IN *A 31-DAY EXPERIENCE: THE PURSUIT OF GOD*

I make it my business only to persevere in His holy presence, wherein I keep myself by a simple attention, and a general fond regard to *God*, which I may call an actual presence of *God;* or, to speak better, an habitual, silent, and secret conversation of the soul with *God*, which often causes in me joys and raptures inwardly, and sometimes also outwardly, so great that I am forced to use means to moderate them, and prevent their appearance to others.

In short, I am assured beyond all doubt, that my soul has been with *God* above these thirty years. I pass over many things, that I may not be tedious to you, yet I think it proper to inform you after what manner I consider myself before *God*, whom I behold as my King.

I consider myself as the most wretched of men, full of sores and corruption, and who has committed all sorts of crimes against his King; touched with a sensible regret I confess to Him all my wickedness, I ask His forgiveness, I abandon myself in His hands, that He may do what He pleases with me. This King, full of mercy and goodness, very far from chastising me, embraces me with love, makes me eat at His table, serves me with His own hands, gives me the key of His treasures; He converses and delights Himself with me incessantly, in a thousand and a thousand ways, and treats me in all respects as His favourite. It is thus I consider myself from time to time in His holy presence. My most usual method is this simple attention, and such a general passionate regard to *God*; to whom I find myself often attached with greater sweetness and delight than that of an infant at the mother's breast: so that if I dare use the expression, I should choose to call this state the bosom of *God,* for the inexpressible sweetness which I taste and experience there.[3]

BROTHER LAWRENCE IN *THE PRACTICE OF THE PRESENCE OF GOD*

The test of a man's religious life and character is not what he does in the exceptional moments of life, but what he does in the ordinary times, when there is nothing tremendous or exciting on. The worth of a man is revealed in his attitude to ordinary things when he is not before the footlights (cf. John 1:36). It is a painful business to get through into the stride of God, it means getting your second wind spiritually. In learning to walk with God there is always the difficulty of getting into His stride, but when we have got into it, the only characteristic that manifests itself is the life of God. The individual man is lost sight of in his personal union with God, and the stride and the power of God alone are manifested.[4]

OSWALD CHAMBERS IN *MY UTMOST FOR HIS HIGHEST*

ENJOY HIS PRESENCE

The Bible encourages you to walk by faith. If this is the case, then how can *knowing* God occur in your life experience? Experience seems to be the opposite of faith. This is not so in God's economy. Faith in God and His Word is lived out in everyday life. It is a *by-faith experience.*

God will show you truth about His character and ways in His Word. What will you do with what He shows you? Will you launch out and take action? If so, you will see God at work and you will come to know Him more intimately.

As you close your time with the Lord today, think about what you have learned about knowing God. How are you experiencing the presence of God in your life? In what ways are you resting on the truth of God's Word, moment by moment, rather than on what you feel or see? As you do that, how are you seeing the reality of God lived out in your own life? Record your thoughts. Close by talking with the Lord about what you have learned today. Tell Him your desire to know Him more.

REST IN HIS LOVE

"So let us know, let us press on to know the LORD.
His going forth is as certain as the dawn;
And He will come to us like the rain,
Like the spring rain watering the earth." (Hosea 6:3)

God — the relentless romancer

Be still, and know that I am . . .
PSALM 46:10, NIV

Prepare Your Heart

One of the most profound discoveries the child of God makes in the adventure of knowing God is that He is a personal God. He romances those He loves. He constantly woos them to Himself. He has a relationship with a wonderful future for His people. It is an amazing fact that God, the Creator of the universe, has actually chosen to reach out of heaven and speak to those He has created. He romances not just people in general but also individuals. He is intensely interested in you. He wants to dance with you. Once you realize this, your life will never be the same. You will launch out to know Him with renewed fervency.

God is relentless in His pursuit of you and me. He never gives up. He will never quit. He has been called the hound of heaven. And what a great thing that is. You and I would never choose God for ourselves if He did not choose us first and romance us, meeting us at every turn. Can you imagine that our hearts can be so deceived that we would not choose that one thing that is highest and truest and best! And yet our God is so gracious and compassionate, filled with a boundless love that constantly initiates a relationship of intimacy and joy. And what does He want to give us? Himself. The riches of heaven. Fellowship with the Lord Jesus Christ, our Savior. Eternal life. "THINGS WHICH EYE HAS NOT SEEN AND EAR HAS NOT HEARD, AND WHICH HAVE NOT ENTERED THE HEART OF MAN, ALL THAT GOD HAS PREPARED FOR THOSE WHO LOVE HIM" (1 Corinthians 2:9).

Never forget God's great love for you. He is always present, always desiring intimacy with you. Isn't that what you have always wanted: someone who would love you with a reckless abandon, who would do what it takes to meet every need in your life with Himself?

As you begin your time with the Lord today, turn to Psalm 8 and meditate on the words written by David, the man after God's own heart. Have you realized that the Lord takes thought and notice of you? Do you know that He has a plan for you? Are you prepared today to hear what He has to say to you? As you read Psalm 8, record your insights.

READ AND STUDY GOD'S WORD

1. Read Psalm 46 again. Note the context of all that is said in this psalm. Psalm 46 seems to list all that we should know and do in a time of trouble. As you read through it, what do you read about God that encourages you? What actions does the psalm encourage you to take? In what ways do you see that God is a personal God to you, a relentless romancer, and is intensely interested in you no matter what you are experiencing in life?

God is our refuge & strength
He is always with us.

2. Scripture repeatedly reveals God's heart of love and compassion. No matter what your sin, no matter how far you have wandered, the Lord continues to love you and will break through to woo you to Himself. What does He desire? You. He wants your love. Look at the following verses and record what you learn about the heart of God.

Deuteronomy 4:23-39

Deuteronomy 7:7-9

Isaiah 49:14-16

Isaiah 61:3,10-11

Isaiah 65:1

Jeremiah 3:6-23

Zechariah 2:3-5

Zechariah 2:8

Zechariah 3:1-5

1 John 4:16-19

Revelation 19:7-8; 21:3-4; 22:3-4

3. How has God made Himself known to you? How have you seen Him work in your own life? In what ways have you seen Him pursuing you as the relentless Romancer?

ADORE GOD IN PRAYER

Make today a day of thanksgiving to the Lord for the ways He has worked in your life. As the hymn says, "Count your many blessings, name them one by one." You may even wish to write a prayer of thanksgiving in your Journal, expressing all that is on your heart.

YIELD YOURSELF TO GOD

God is a person, and in the deep of His mighty nature He thinks, wills, enjoys, feels, loves, desires and suffers as any other person may. In making Himself known to us He stays by the familiar pattern of personality. He communicates with us through the avenues of our minds, our wills and our emotions. The continuous and unembarrassed interchange of love and thought between God and the soul of the redeemed man is the throbbing heart of New Testament religion.[1]

A. W. TOZER IN *THE PURSUIT OF GOD*

Have you not found the gospel to be in yourselves just what the Bible said it would be? Jesus said He would give you rest—have you not enjoyed the sweetest peace in Him? He said you should have joy, and comfort, and life through believing in Him—have you not received all these? Are not His ways, ways of pleasantness, and His paths, paths of peace? Surely you can say with the queen of Sheba, *The half has not been told me.* I have found Christ more sweet than His servants ever said He was. I looked upon His likeness as they painted it, but it was a mere daub compared with Himself; for the King in His beauty outshines all imaginable loveliness. Surely what we have *seen* keeps pace with, nay, far exceeds, what we have *heard.* Let us, then glorify and praise God for a Savior so precious, and so satisfying.[2]

CHARLES SPURGEON IN *MORNING AND EVENING*

ENJOY HIS PRESENCE

As you close your time with the Lord, think about your relationship with Him. It is to be at the highest and deepest level: that of an intimate partnership between the beloved and the lover. In the Bible, God is the Pursuer, the Romancer, the Lover. You are the pursued, the romanced, the beloved.

Draw near to the Lord now. Meditate on these words by Amy Carmichael.

One thing have I desired, my God, of Thee,
That will I seek, Thine house be home to me.
I would not breathe an alien, other air,
I would be with Thee, O Thou fairest Fair.

For I would see the beauty of my Lord,
And hear Him speak, who is my heart's Adored.
O Love of loves, and can such wonder dwell
In Thy great Name of names, Immanuel?
Thou with Thy child, Thy child at home with Thee,
O Love of loves, I love, I worship Thee.[3]

Rest in His Love

There is a river whose streams make glad the city of God,
The holy dwelling places of the Most High.
God is in the midst of her, she will not be moved;
God will help her when morning dawns. (Psalm 46:4-5)

everything necessary

... know that I am God.
PSALM 46:10

Prepare Your Heart

In the midst of trial and trouble that won't go away, what will encourage you not to give up? What will comfort you and carry you through? It must be something that has more power than the present circumstance. The only One who possesses such strength is your God. That is really what God is saying in Psalm 46:10. In the midst of trouble, He is your refuge and strength. Even though everything around you is changing, God is there. And the great encouragement, the truth that no trouble can shake, is that God is enough. He is everything you need. He has a plan even when no future is in sight. He has a comfort even in an incurable trial. He has hope and a future even when there is nothing left. Still there is God. He is enough. No matter what.

Amy Carmichael discovered this truth when she spent the last twenty years of her life as an invalid due to an accident. Corrie ten Boom discovered it as she endured the horrors of Ravensbruck concentration camp. J. Hudson Taylor made this truth his own when he went to China and became so ill and homesick that he thought he could not go on. There is a long list, a "great cloud of witnesses" who have faced the unthinkable and the impossible, and have discovered that He is God. The reality of that one truth is force enough to turn the tide in any situation.

You are going to spend the weeks ahead looking at the lives of men and women of God who experienced many different circumstances. They all came to know and love God in an intimate relationship. One thing you will notice: at some point in their lives, they experienced the trial that threatened to capsize them into unending despair. What did they do? They stopped everything. *Be still.* And they turned all their attention toward one thing: God. They drew near. *And know that I am God.* This, dear friends, is one of the greatest secrets in

developing intimacy with your God. In the crucible of life, the fiery trial, what will you do?
God is present in you. Will you draw near? If so, you are on the road to an intimate relationship that nothing in this world can ever touch. The apostle Paul wrote, "In all these things we
overwhelmingly conquer through Him who loved us. For I am convinced that neither death,
nor life, nor angels, nor principalities, nor things present, nor things to come, nor powers,
nor height, nor depth, nor any other created thing, will be able to separate us from the love
of God, which is in Christ Jesus our Lord" (Romans 8:37-39).

If something in your life right now is threatening to crush you, just know that He is God.
It is always too soon to give up. Jesus is always the answer in every situation of life. He is
always the way through the storm. Today, in preparation for your time alone with God, ask
the Lord to speak to your heart.

Read and Study God's Word

1. *Elohim* means Almighty God. The name is often used in the Bible to mark the contrast
between God and man. *Elohim* is Creator, wholly Other, uncreated, supreme, sovereign,
and in control of all things. If you will fix your eyes on Him, *Elohim*, you will discover that
your troubles will seem less ominous to you. Your circumstances don't go away, but some-
how your great God fills your view. The circumstances don't loom as large, nor do they
hold the same power. God's greatness does not minimize the severity of certain losses or
troubles in life. Yet God is a great God, and there is comfort and healing to be found in
Him if only you will run to Him. Look at the following verses and record your insights
related to God and any encouragement you find for the trials of life. Be sure to personalize
your answers.

Deuteronomy 1:29-31

Joshua 1:9

1 Chronicles 29:10-13

Ezra 9:9

Job 37:22-24

Psalm 31:7-8

Psalm 147:2-6

Jeremiah 10:6

Jeremiah 32:17,26-27

2. Which truth about God is your favorite today and why?

ADORE GOD IN PRAYER

Lord, High and Holy, Meek and Lowly,
Thou hast brought me to the valley of vision,
Where I live in the depths, but see Thee in the heights;
Hemmed in by mountains of sin I behold Thy glory.
Let me learn by paradox
That the way down is the way up,
That to be low is to be high,
That the broken heart is the healed heart,
That the contrite spirit is the rejoicing spirit,
That the repenting soul is the victorious soul,
That to have nothing is to possess all,
That to bear the cross is to wear the crown,
That to give is to receive,
That the valley is the place of vision.

Lord, in the daytime stars can be seen from deepest wells,
And the deeper the wells the brighter thy stars shine;
Let me find thy light in my darkness,
Thy life in my death,
Thy joy in my sorrow,
Thy grace in my sin,
Thy glory in my valley.[1]

ARTHUR BENNETT IN *THE VALLEY OF VISION*

YIELD YOURSELF TO GOD

So often discouragement comes from believing that which is not true. In doing so, we are
deceived. Despair can set in when we begin to interpret God by our circumstances and
ascribe things to Him that do not line up with what is true in His Word. That is why there
is only one way to look at God: by what He says in His Word. Part of the divine romance
with God involves knowing and understanding God as He really is. Once God's people
realize what is true, they are set free to love and serve Him. Perhaps you have felt abandoned by God at times. Maybe you have even thought that God may choose others, but
He has not chosen you. The adversity is so great that there is no external proof that He
loves you.

It is important to stop and think about what will determine your understanding of God's
character. Will it be your external circumstances or what God says in His Word? Decide this
once and for all. If you choose His Word, then you will have a strong, steadfast foundation
that cannot be shaken. And you will find yourself on the road to a certain and blessed intimacy with God. Read the words of Hannah Whitall Smith in *The God of All Comfort* as she
shares her own discovery of this very thing:

I shall never forget the hour when I first discovered that God was really good. I had,
of course, always known that the Bible said He was good, but I had thought it only
meant He was religiously good; and it had never dawned on me that it meant He was
actually and practically good, with the same kind of goodness He has commanded us
to have . . . and then one day I came in my reading of the Bible across the words, O
taste and see that the Lord is good, and suddenly they meant something. The Lord is good,
I repeated to myself. What does it mean to be good? What but this, the living up to
the best and highest that one knows . . . and I saw that, since God is omniscient, He
must know what is the best and highest good of all, and that therefore His goodness
must necessarily be beyond question. I can never express what this meant to me. I had
such a view of the actual goodness of God that I saw nothing could possibly go wrong
under His care, and it seemed to me that no one could ever be anxious again. And over
and over, when appearances have been against Him, and when I have been tempted to
question whether He had not been unkind, or neglectful, or indifferent, I have been

brought up short by the words, *the Lord is good*, and I have seen that it was simply unthinkable that a God who was good could have done the bad things I had imagined.

The Bible is not an end in itself, but a means to bring men to an intimate and satisfying knowledge of God, that they may enter into Him, that they may delight in His Presence, may taste and know the inner sweetness of the very God Himself in the core and center of their hearts.[2]

A. W. TOZER IN THE PURSUIT OF GOD

In Romans 8:31, Paul points out that if God is for you, who can possibly be against you? Meditate on these words by John Piper in *The Pleasures of God:*

God will not turn away from doing you good. He will keep on doing good. He doesn't do good to his children sometimes and bad to them other times. He keeps on doing good and he never will stop doing good for ten thousand ages of ages. When things are going *bad* that does not mean God has stopped doing *good*. It means he is shifting things around to get them in place for more good, if you will go on loving him. He works all things together for good *for those who love him* (Romans 8:28). *No good thing does he withhold from those who walk uprightly* (Psalm 84:11). *Lo, it was for my welfare that I had great bitterness* (Isaiah 38:17). *It is good for me that I was afflicted, that I might learn your statutes* (Psalm 119:71).[3]

The old mystics used to teach what they called *detachment,* meaning the cutting loose of the soul from all that could hold it back from God. This need for detachment is the secret of many of our *shakings.* We cannot follow the Lord fully so long as we are tied fast to anything else, any more than a boat can sail out into the boundless ocean so long as it is tied fast to the shore. . . . When everything in our lives and experience is shaken that can be shaken, and only that which cannot be shaken remains, we are brought to see that God only is our rock and our foundation, and we learn to have our expectation from Him alone.

HANNAH WHITALL SMITH IN THE GOD OF ALL COMFORT

Do you see the heart of God who longs to have you for His own? It is the Divine Romance. The God of the universe desires that you know Him and enjoy intimacy with Him. He is everything for you, and He is enough for every situation of life. Don't hold back, even in the midst of great adversity! "Draw near to God and He will draw near to you" (James 4:8).

ENJOY HIS PRESENCE

Take some time now to "be still and know" that He is God. If you have any troubles or worries that are threatening to steal your rest in the Lord, take time in the stillness of these moments and think about the greatness of your God. Run to Him. Find your refuge, your safety, your very life in Him.

As you close your time with the Lord, meditate on these words of Amy Carmichael. She discovered the secret of God. Have you?

> O Thou beloved child of My desire,
> Whether I lead thee through green valleys,
> By still waters,
> Or through fire,
> Or lay thee down in silence under snow,
> Through any weather, and whatever
> Cloud may gather,
> Wind may blow—
> Wilt love Me? Trust Me? Praise Me?
>
> No gallant bird, O dearest Lord, am I,
> That anywhere, in any weather,
> Rising singeth;
> Low I lie.
> And yet I cannot fear, for I shall soar,
> Thy love shall wing me, blessed Saviour;
> So I answer,
> I adore,
> I love Thee, trust Thee, praise Thee.[4]

REST IN HIS LOVE
"Behold, I am the LORD, the God of all flesh; is anything too difficult for Me?" (Jeremiah 32:27).

Dear Friend,

The next two days are your opportunity to spend time reviewing what you have learned this week. You may wish to write your thoughts and insights in your Journal or the Journal Pages in the back of this book. As you think about God's invitation to an intimate relationship with you, record:

Your most significant insight:

Your favorite quote:

Your favorite verse:

Close this week by meditating on these words by Hannah Whitall Smith in *The Christian's Secret of a Happy Life.*

It seems to me just in this way: as though Christ were living in a house, shut up in a far-off closet, unknown and unnoticed by the dwellers in the house, longing to make Himself known to them, and to be one with them in all their daily lives, and share in all their interests, but unwilling to force Himself upon their notice, because nothing but a voluntary companionship could meet or satisfy the needs of His love. The days pass by over that favored household, and they remain in ignorance of their marvelous privilege. They come and go about all their daily affairs, with no thought of their wonderful Guest. Their plans are laid without reference to Him. His wisdom to guide and His strength to protect are all lost to them. Lonely days and weeks are spent in sadness which might have been full of the sweetness of His presence. But suddenly the announcement is made: *The Lord is in the house!* How will its owner receive the intelligence? Will he call out an eager thanksgiving, and throw wide open every door for the entrance of his glorious Guest? Or will he shrink and hesitate, afraid of His presence, and seek to reserve some private corner for a refuge from His all-seeing eye? Dear friend, I make the glad announcement to you that the Lord is in your heart. Since the day of your conversion He has been dwelling there, but you have lived on in ignorance of it. Every moment during all that time might have been passed in the sunshine of His sweet presence, and every step might have been taken under His advice. But because you did not know it, and did not look for Him there, your life has been lonely and full of failure. But now that I make the announcement to you, how will you receive it? Are you glad to have Him? Will you throw wide open every door to welcome Him in? Will you joyfully and thankfully give up the government of your life into His hands? Will you consult Him about everything, and let Him decide each step for you, and mark out every path? Will you invite Him into your innermost chambers, and make Him the sharer in your most hidden life? Will you say *yes* to all His longing for union with you, and with a glad and eager abandonment hand yourself and all that concerns you over into His hands? If you will, then shall your soul begin to know something of the joy of union with Christ.[1]

journey to the heart of God

week
two

HOSEA

the broken heart

"Go, take to yourself a wife of harlotry and have children of harlotry;
for the land commits flagrant harlotry, forsaking the LORD."

HOSEA 1:2

Prepare Your Heart

Once you embark on the adventure of intimacy with God, you will begin to "taste and see," as the psalmist said, "that the LORD is good" (Psalm 34:8). As you go deeper into the territory of His love, then you begin the journey on a road where few dare to go. It is, at times, a painful climb, but the views and the landscape are incomparable. This is the journey to the heart of God.

Not every believer enters into this sacred place. Many stop at the threshold. Why? Because at the threshold, in almost every case, is the experience of the broken, wounded heart—God's heart and your own. Brokenness—not something any would invite. Yet you cannot escape it if you would know God.

God is wounded over the sin and evil that His people become involved in. These offend Him because of His holiness and righteousness. If you would venture near to the heart of God, you will be wounded by the sin around you, sometimes even by those you love very much. In this way, you share the broken heart of God. You will discover this week that sharing God's heart involves so much. You begin to dream His dreams and are filled with His desires. It is a great joy to be able to love with His love and forgive with His forgiveness. That is what the journey to His heart is all about.

The prophets of God were called to share God's heart. Jeremiah was called to preach a message from God that broke his own heart. He said, "Oh, that my head were waters and my eyes a fountain of tears, that I might weep day and night for the slain of the daughter of my people!" (Jeremiah 9:1). He was called the weeping prophet.

God called Ezekiel to be a living object lesson for His people. God asked him to do many things, such as shave his head, as signs of what would happen to God's people. Ezekiel experienced what God was feeling about the people's disobedience and idolatry.

One prophet who probably felt God's breaking heart more than any other was Hosea. God called him to love a wife who was a prostitute. In doing so, Hosea journeyed to the depths of God's heart. What he felt there gave him an intimacy with God that few have known.

God is calling you to the privilege of sharing His heart. Will you journey there? If so, then you will begin to truly dance with Him. This week, as you look at Hosea's life, you will see many facets of your Lord's heart.

Today, as you draw near to God, turn to Psalm 34 and meditate on the words. What do you see about intimacy and sharing life with your Lord?

READ AND STUDY GOD'S WORD

Hosea lived during the time when the kingdoms were divided into the southern kingdom of Judah and the northern kingdom of Israel. Hosea prophesied to the northern kingdom at the same time that Isaiah and Micah prophesied to the southern kingdom. In fact, Hosea was the last prophet to the northern kingdom before the Assyrians took the Israelites into captivity.

Hosea married a woman named Gomer. Somewhere along the way, she made a decision to commit adultery and broke her husband's heart. In those days Gomer's actions were punishable by death. Yet Hosea loved his wife. What should he do? God made it clear. Hosea, an intimate friend of God, chose the journey to the heart of God. It began with a broken heart.

1. Read Hosea 1 and describe all that God asked Hosea to do.

to help Gomer

2. How difficult do you think it was for Hosea to do what God asked of him? What qualities were required of Hosea in order to do what God asked?

3. What did God want Hosea's actions to illustrate?

obedience
forgiveness

4. In Hosea 13:1-6, in what ways do you see God's broken heart over His people's behavior?

5. Look at the following verses and record your insights about how suffering can be the path to intimacy with God. Remember the promise: "Weeping may go on all night, but joy comes with the morning" (Psalm 30:5, NLT).

Romans 8:16-18

2 Corinthians 1:5

Philippians 3:10-11

1 Peter 4:12-14

6. We suffer deeply when the ones we love wound our heart. Your heart may be broken by a spouse, child, parent, or friend. Peter said that "those also who suffer according to the will of God shall entrust their souls to a faithful Creator in doing what is right" (1 Peter 4:19). He also used the example of a wife who lives with a husband who is disobedient to the Word. He said such husbands may be "won without a word by the behavior of their wives" (1 Peter 3:1). One of the best examples of one who lived with a difficult man is Abigail. Oh what an intimate of God she was! Abigail was a valiant warrior who truly shared the broken heart of God. She was married to Nabal, who is described as harsh and evil in his dealings. Surely, in the private moments, she suffered great pain. God honored

her in the midst of a difficult situation and gave her wisdom and strength. Read the story of Abigail in 1 Samuel 25:1-42. What is your favorite part of this true story?

ADORE GOD IN PRAYER

Pray the words of this prayer from Jeremiah 17:14. You may want to write it on a three-by-five card, memorize it, and pray these words to the Lord throughout the day.

> Heal me, O LORD, and I will be healed;
> Save me and I will be saved,
> For You are my praise.

YIELD YOURSELF TO GOD

"In the shadow of his hand hath he hid me, and made me a polished shaft; in his quiver hath he hid me" (Isaiah 49:2, KJV). In the shadow. We must all go there sometimes. The glare of the daylight is too brilliant; our eyes are injured and unable to discern the delicate shades of color, or appreciate neutral tints—the shadowed chamber of sickness, the shadowed house of mourning, the shadowed life from which the sunlight has gone. But fear not! It is the shadow of God's hand. He is leading you. There are lessons that can be learned only there.

> The photograph of His face can only be fixed in the dark chamber. But do not suppose that He has cast thee aside. Thou art still in His quiver; He has not flung thee away as a worthless thing. He is only keeping thee close till the moment comes when He can send thee most swiftly and surely on some errand in which He will be glorified. Oh, shadowed, solitary ones, remember how closely the quiver is bound to the warrior, within easy reach of the hand, and guarded jealously. (*Christ in Isaiah*, Meyer)
>
> In some spheres the shadow condition is the condition of greatest growth. The beautiful Indian corn never grows more rapidly than in the shadow of a warm summer night. The sun curls the leaves in the sultry noon light, but they quickly unfold, if a cloud slips over the sky. There is a service in the shadow that is not in the shine. The world of stellar beauty is never seen at its best till the shadows of night slip over the sky. There are beauties that bloom in the shade that will not bloom in the sun. There

is much greenery in lands of fog and clouds and shadow. The florist has evening glories now, as well as morning glories. The evening glory will not shine in the noon's splendor, but comes to its best as the shadows of evening deepen.[1]

Mrs. Charles Cowman in Streams in the Desert

Remember the ship that was tossed by the storm on the Galilean lake? There was certainly a dreary outlook for that boat. Before long, the ship would have been driven against the rocky shore and would have sunk beneath the waves. But this was not the case, for walking on the waves, which hardened to glass beneath His feet, was the Man who loved the group of men on that boat, and He would not allow them to die. It was Jesus, walking on the waves of the sea. He came into the vessel, and immediately the calm was as profound as if no wave had risen against the boat and no wind had blown.

In the same way, in the darkest times of the church's history, Jesus has, in due time, always appeared walking on the waves of her troubles, and then her rest has been glorious. Let us not, therefore, be afraid. Instead, throwing fear aside, let us rejoice with the most joyful expectation. What can there be to fear? *God is with us* (Isaiah 8:10). Is that phrase not the battle cry before which demons flee and all the hosts of evil turn their backs? *Emmanuel . . . God with us* (Matthew 1:23). Who dares to stand against that? Who will defy the Lion of the tribe of Judah? They can bring their might and their spears, but if God is for us, who can be against us? Or if any are against us, how can they stand? God is our own God. Will He let His own church be trampled in the mire? Will the bride of Christ be led into captivity? Will His beloved, whom He bought with blood, be delivered into the hands of her enemies? God forbid! Because He is God, because He is for us, because He is our own God, we set up our banners and each of us cheerfully sings:

> For yet I know I shall Him praise,
> Who graciously to me
> The health is of my countenance,
> Yea, mine own God is He.[2]

Charles Spurgeon in Spurgeon on Prayer and Spiritual Warfare

Enjoy His Presence

In what way are you sharing the heart of God that is broken by the sin of His people? Is there a place of suffering for you that causes you pain? Press through that pain by faith in Christ alone, and draw near to the Lord today. He will draw near to you with arms open wide and healing words of comfort for your soul. You may wish to write a prayer to the Lord in your Journal, expressing all that is on your heart.

Lord God of gardens who in love disposes
Sun, rain, wind violent,
So that our bushes flower to Thee in roses
We are content.
We do not ask to choose our garden's weather,
Too ignorant are we.
Only that we Thy gardeners together
May pleasure Thee.[3]

AMY CARMICHAEL IN GOLD BY MOONLIGHT

REST IN HIS LOVE

"The sacrifices of God are a broken spirit; a broken and a contrite heart, O God, You will not despise" (Psalm 51:17).

the winsome heart

"I am now going to allure her;
I will lead her into the desert and speak tenderly to her."
HOSEA 2:14, NIV

Prepare Your Heart

As you share God's heart, it will soon become apparent to you that some around you do not choose to take the journey. In fact, some are apathetic to the journey. Others are openly antagonistic to the truth of God's Word and any kind of relationship with God. Paul tells us, "Our struggle is not against flesh and blood, but against the rulers, against the powers, against the world forces of this darkness, against the spiritual forces of wickedness in the heavenly places" (Ephesians 6:12). Those who do not love God are deceived by the Enemy and his followers. This is something you must know and recall to mind often, especially when those you love are not following the Lord. It is a spiritual battle.

This was especially important for the prophets to understand. They were called to speak forth God's Word to an immoral, idolatrous, and often godless generation. In Hosea's time, the people of God had completely forgotten the Lord and were immersed in their own aimless pursuits. We come then to the heart of God. How did He respond? Did He wipe out those faithless ones? No. He said, "I am now going to allure her; I will lead her into the desert and speak tenderly to her" (Hosea 2:14).

In these words you see how God is completely different from man. God's heart is winsome. He desires to woo you and draw you to Himself. God wears His heart on His sleeve. You will see it over and over again in the things He says to His people. God draws His wayward children to Himself with love and grace. Grace does not excuse disobedience. God will deal with that. But He is a God of mercy. And while His wrath is kindled by sin and evil, He knows man's frame. He formed man from the dust of the ground. His primary way of dealing with sin is by paying the penalty for it Himself. This is an incomprehensible truth that will make you fall on your knees if you attempt to wrap your mind around it. His love is so great that He sent His only Son, Jesus, to die on the cross for the sins of His created beings. He went beyond the scope of human reason to reach out to wicked, defiant people that they might turn and choose Him. Paul said, "Whenever a person turns to the Lord, the veil is taken away" (2 Corinthians 3:16). That is what the Lord is waiting for. If one who has turned his or her back on the truth will entertain the possibility of God's ways and His existence, that veil will lift by the power of the Holy Spirit. The Lord loves to reveal Himself to His people.

Today, your goal is to meditate on the Lord's ways. You want to understand God's winsome, beautiful, gracious heart. In doing so, you will change forever how you deal with people who cause you pain. You will see that revenge and anger and self-pity are out of the question. In sharing God's heart, you constantly reach out in love to those around you. To do so requires an intimacy with God that perhaps you have not known before. It means stepping completely outside of yourself and your own needs and desires, and finding your satisfaction completely in God Himself. Your actions will no longer depend on feelings and circumstances, but on the truth found in God's Word. You will depend on His character and ways for the choices you make in life.

As you think about these things, turn to the Lord now. Write a prayer, asking God to reveal Himself to you. Tell Him how much you want to know Him and His ways.

READ AND STUDY GOD'S WORD

1. To understand the depth of God's love and His response to His people's actions, it is important for you to see what His people were doing. Read Hosea 2:1-13 and record the actions of the people that offended God.

2. In what ways do people do the same kinds of things today?

3. God said that the nation of Israel followed other lovers (see Hosea 2:13) and forgot Him. God's response to that behavior reveals a heart that truly loves His people. Read Hosea 2:14-23. Which phrase means the most to you today?

4. Look more closely at Hosea 2:14. What is it about a desert or wilderness experience in the life of a believer that makes it easier to hear God speak? Describe what you notice about the desert.

Quiet -peaceful

What does the phrase "allure her" or "lead her" tell you about the heart and character of God?

5. Read Hosea 14 and record how, once again, you see the winsome heart of the Lord wooing His people to Himself.

6. In what way was Hosea called to share God's winsome heart?

7. Look at the following verses and record what you learn about how God's ways can become a part of our own manner of dealing with people. Personalize your answers. For example, "*I* will not speak evil of another. The Lord will vindicate *me*."
    Proverbs 20:22

    Romans 12:16-21

⅄   Colossians 4:5-6

1 Peter 3:1-17

8. Summarize in one or two sentences what you have learned about God's heart and His ways today.

ADORE GOD IN PRAYER
Turn to your Lord in prayer and offer up those situations in your life where you need His winsome heart. You may want to record your requests on the Prayer Pages in the back of this book.

YIELD YOURSELF TO GOD
Meditate on the following words about the grace of God found in William R. Newell's book, *Romans, Verse by Verse.* Return to them often, for they are filled with principles based on the truth of God's Word. You will see different facets of the winsome heart of a God who draws His people to Himself. As you learn God's truth, you will be set free to love and serve Him.

A Few Words About Grace

THE NATURE OF GRACE
1. Grace is God acting freely, according to His own nature as Love; with no promises or obligations to fulfill; and acting, of course, righteously — in view of the cross.
2. Grace, therefore is *uncaused* in the recipient: its cause lies wholly in the *Giver*, in *God*.
3. Grace, also is *sovereign*. Not having debts to pay, or fulfilled conditions on man's part to wait for, it can act toward whom, and how, it pleases. It can, and does, often, place the worst deservers in the highest favors.

4. Grace cannot act where there is either *desert* or *ability*: grace does not *help*—it is *absolute, it does all.*

5. There being *no cause* in the creature why Grace should be shown, the creature must be brought off from *trying to give cause* to God for His Grace.

6. The discovery by the creature that he is truly the object of Divine grace, works the *utmost humility*: for the receiver of grace is brought to know his own absolute unworthiness, and his complete inability to attain worthiness: yet he finds himself blessed—*on another principle, outside of himself!*

7. Therefore, *flesh has no place* in the plan of Grace. This is *the great reason why Grace is hated* by the proud natural mind of man. But for this very reason, the true believer rejoices! For he knows that *in him, that is, his flesh, is no good thing;* and yet he finds God glad to bless him, just as he is!

THE PLACE OF MAN UNDER GRACE

1. He has been accepted *in Christ*, who *is* his standing!

2. He is not "on probation."

3. As to his life past, *it does not exist* before God: he *died* at the Cross, and *Christ is his life.*

4. Grace, once bestowed, is *not withdrawn*: for God knew all the human exigencies beforehand: His action was independent of them, not dependent upon them.

5. The failure of devotion does not cause the withdrawal of bestowed grace (as it would under law).

THE PROPER ATTITUDE OF MAN UNDER GRACE

1. To *believe*, and to consent to be *loved while unworthy*, is the great secret.

2. To refuse to make "resolutions" and "vows"; for that is to trust in the flesh.

3. To expect to be blessed, though realizing more and more lack of worth.

4. To testify of God's goodness, at all times.

5. To be certain of God's future favor; yet to be ever more tender in conscience toward Him.

6. To rely on God's chastening hand as a mark of His kindness.

7. A man under grace, if like Paul, has no burdens regarding himself; but many about others.

THINGS WHICH GRACIOUS SOULS DISCOVER

1. To "hope to be better" is to fail to see yourself *in Christ only*.

2. To be *disappointed* with yourself, is to have *believed* in yourself.

3. To be *discouraged* is unbelief—as to God's purpose and plan of blessing for you.

4. To be *proud*, is to be *blind!* For we have no standing before God, in *ourselves*.

5. The lack of Divine blessing, therefore, comes from *unbelief*, and not from *failure of devotion*.

6. Real *devotion* to God arises, not from *man's will* to show it; but from the discovery that blessing *has been received* from God while we were yet *unworthy and undevoted*.

7. To preach devotion first, and blessing second, is to reverse God's order, and preach *law, not grace*. The Law made man's blessing depend on devotion; Grace *confers undeserved, unconditional* blessing: our devotion may follow, but does not always do so, in proper measure.

As you read these truths about grace and the winsome, kind heart of God, what is your favorite insight and why? You may even wish to write a prayer to the Lord in response to what you have read about His grace.

ENJOY HIS PRESENCE

Can you think of situations in your own life where you need this gracious heart of God to reach out to others around you? In what ways can you demonstrate His love and grace and forgiveness today?

REST IN HIS LOVE

"To sum up, all of you be harmonious, sympathetic, brotherly, kindhearted, and humble in spirit; not returning evil for evil or insult for insult, but giving a blessing instead; for you were called for the very purpose that you might inherit a blessing" (1 Peter 3:8-9).

the faithful heart

"Go again, love a woman who is loved by her husband, yet an adulteress,
even as the LORD loves the sons of Israel, though they turn
to other gods and love raisin cakes."

HOSEA 3:1

Prepare Your Heart

Polycarp was born in A.D. 70. The apostle John appointed him as bishop of Smyrna, and by the end of Polycarp's life, he was the last surviving disciple of one of the original twelve apostles. He championed the faith and opposed enemies of Christ and heresies such as Gnosticism. He encouraged the churches, writing letters to exhort them in their service for Christ.

While he lived an exemplary life for Jesus Christ, his death revealed the depths of his faithfulness. At that time, believers were being persecuted and martyred for their faith. During some pagan festivals in Smyrna, eleven Christians were dragged into the stadium to be thrown to wild beasts. After the eleven died, the crowd demanded Polycarp's death because he was the most well-known, faithful follower of Christ in that region.

The Roman soldiers arrested him, and Polycarp was challenged to revile Christ. He made his stand by exclaiming, "For eighty-six years I have been his servant, and he has done me no wrong. How can I blaspheme my King who saved me?" Following these words, Polycarp was declared a Christian and condemned to death by fire. The account of his execution records that he was tied to the stake and surrounded by flames, yet the fire did not touch him. Therefore, the executioner was ordered to kill Polycarp with a dagger.

This is just one man's story. Countless others have given up their earthly lives because of faithfulness to Jesus Christ: John and Betty Stam, William Tyndale, Betsie ten Boom . . . While most of us will never be called upon to die a martyr's death for Christ, we are all called to live the life of devotion that these people displayed, a life of reckless abandonment to the will of God.

It is said that an old Roman coin displayed an altar on one side and a plow on the other. The inscription read, "Ready for either." Today, ask God to deepen your devotion to Him and give you a fresh perspective of your relationship with Christ. You may wish to write a prayer below.

READ AND STUDY GOD'S WORD

Today you are going to look at one of the main themes in the book of Hosea: *faithfulness*. You will learn what it is to share in God's faithful heart. In Hosea's journey to the heart of God, he shared in this quality. He was married to an adulteress. God asked him to pursue her, not to give up on her. How painful this must have been to Hosea's heart. And how painful it must be to God when His people are silent toward Him, never sharing in His life. Yet He is faithful. He continues to reach out to His people.

1. Read Hosea 3. Record what you learn about God's faithfulness and Hosea's faithfulness. What actions did they take as a result of faithfulness?

Hosea 14

Hosea 2:14-23 describes the kind of relationship God desired with His people. In verse 16, the word *Ishi* means "my husband" and the word *Baali* means "my master." According to the customs of the day, betrothal was as binding as marriage. In a betrothal the bride and groom were officially pledged to each other, but the marriage was not yet consummated. Betrothal provided for most of the legal rights of marriage and was established by two witnesses, mutual consent, and the groom's declaration. It was even more binding than an engagement and could only be terminated by divorce. Complete loyalty and devotion was required from both parties. In the Hebrew culture, if there was infidelity, the injured party was required to expose the other to shame and to terminate the betrothal with divorce. If it was the woman who was unfaithful, she would never find another husband and would have no means of support if her parents died.

2. According to Hosea 2:14-23, what kind of relationship did God desire with His people?

Bless them —

3. What are things in this life that are like the "raisin cakes" or "choice gifts" (NLT) of Hosea 3:1? What are the delicacies of this world? What are the ways that people can commit adultery today in their relationship with the Lord?

4. Are there any "raisin cakes" in your life that you love more than the Lord?

5. Look again at Hosea 3. What will be the result of God's faithfulness in the lives of His people?

6. God asks for the same kind of faithfulness in our lives today. First Corinthians is like a New Testament book of Hosea. There was immorality and unfaithfulness in the Corinthian church. Read 2 Corinthians 11:1-3 and record your insights.

7. Read Ephesians 5:22-27 and describe what Christ has faithfully done for His bride.

8. Why is faithfulness vital to intimacy in a relationship?

9. Do you desire to be faithful to your Lord? How can you demonstrate faithfulness to God today?

Adore God in Prayer
Write a prayer to your Lord today, expressing your love for Him. Thank Him for His faithfulness and love toward you.

Yield Yourself to God

If you have ever loved any of your fellow human beings enough to find sacrifice and service on their behalf a joy; if a whole-souled abandonment of your will to the will of another has ever gleamed across you as a blessed and longed-for privilege, or as a sweet and precious reality, then by all the tender longing love of your Heavenly Lover would I entreat you to let it be so towards Christ. He loves you with more than the love of friendship. As a bridegroom rejoices over his bride, so does He rejoice over you, and nothing but the bride's surrender will satisfy Him. He has given you all, and He asks for all in return. The slightest reserve will grieve Him to the heart. He spared not Himself, and how can you spare yourself? For your sake He poured out in a lavish abandonment all that He had, and for His sake you must pour out all that you have, without stint or measure. Oh, be generous in your self-surrender! Meet His measureless devotion for you with a measureless devotion to Him. Be glad and eager to throw yourself unreservedly into His loving arms, and to hand over the reins of government to Him. Whatever there is of you, let Him have it all. Give up forever everything that is separate from Him. . . . Bring Christ thus into your life and into all its details, and a romance, far grander than the brightest days of youth could ever know, will thrill your soul, and nothing will seem hard or stern again. . . . May our surrendered hearts reach out with an eager delight to discover and embrace the lovely will of our loving God.[1]

HANNAH WHITALL SMITH IN *THE CHRISTIAN'S SECRET OF A HAPPY LIFE*

Will you be wholeheartedly devoted to the Lord today, recklessly abandoned to Him to go where He leads and carry out His desires, pleasing Him in every respect?

ENJOY HIS PRESENCE

Meditate on these words by William R. Newell as you close your time with the Lord today:

There is a faith unmixed with doubt,
A love all free from fear;
A walk with Jesus, where is felt
His presence always near.
There is a rest that God bestows,
Transcending pardon's peace,
A lowly, sweet simplicity,
Where inward conflicts cease.
There is a service God-inspired,
A zeal that tireless grows,
Where self is crucified with Christ,
And joy unceasing flows.
There is a being right with God,
That yields to His commands
Unswerving, true fidelity,
A loyalty that stands.

REST IN HIS LOVE

"I will betroth you to Me forever;
Yes, I will betroth you to Me in righteousness and in justice,
In lovingkindness and in compassion,
And I will betroth you to Me in faithfulness.
Then you will know the LORD." (Hosea 2:19-20)

the discerning heart

My people are destroyed for lack of knowledge.
HOSEA 4:6

Prepare Your Heart

As you go along on this journey to the heart of God and share in His life, you begin to see things as He sees them. You gain the eternal perspective toward circumstances and people. God gives you His discernment. Discernment comes as you spend time in His Word and then live by what you see there. It forever changes your dealings with people and circumstances. Hosea gained such a perspective through his relationship with the Lord, and it enabled him to extend mercy and grace to his wife, Gomer.

As you draw near to the Lord today, meditate on the words of this prayer, asking God to quiet your heart.

My God, I bless thee that thou hast given me the eye of faith,
to see thee as Father,
to know thee as a covenant God,
to experience thy love planted in me;
For faith is the grace of union
By which I spell out my entitlement to thee:
Faith casts my anchor upwards where I trust in thee
And engage thee to be my Lord.
Be pleased to live and move within me,
Breathing in my prayers,
Inhabiting my praises,
Speaking in my words,
Moving in my actions,

Living in my life,
Causing me to grow in grace
Thy bounteous goodness has helped me believe,
But my faith is weak and wavering,
Its light dim,
Its steps tottering,
Its increase slow,
Its backslidings frequent;
It should scale the heavens but lies groveling in the dust.
Lord, fan this divine spark into glowing flame.
When faith sleeps, my heart becomes an unclean thing,
The fount of every loathsome desire,
The cage of unclean lusts
All fluttering to escape,
The noxious tree of deadly fruit,
The open wayside of earthly tares.
Lord, awake faith to put forth its strength
Until all heaven fills my soul
And all impurity is cast out.[1]

FROM *THE VALLEY OF VISION*

READ AND STUDY GOD'S WORD

1. God sees His people's character and actions. This is so apparent in the Old Testament, especially in the words of the prophets. Look at the following verses in Hosea and record what God discerned (understood and distinguished as true) about His people.

Hosea 2:8

Hosea 4:6,10-12

Hosea 5:4

Hosea 8:6-9

Hosea 10:1-2

Hosea 11:7

Summarize in one or two sentences what God saw in His people's lives.

2. Paul wrote about the people of Israel in 1 Corinthians 10:11-14. Record your insights from this passage.

3. As you have looked at the ways of the people of Israel, how has God spoken to you?

ADORE GOD IN PRAYER

Oswald Chambers said discernment is for the purpose of prayer. What has God been showing you recently that perhaps He would like you to bring to Him in your prayer? Take those burdens to the Lord today.

YIELD YOURSELF TO GOD

He setteth an end to darkness (Job 28:3). These words are spoken of the miner who is searching for precious stones, which are buried in the dark mine. He goes into these dark places and lights them, and so ends the darkness—and he finds the jewels hidden there. We are here to do that very thing. We have for light the presence and the promises of God. There may be someone whom we are trying to help; we are trying to bring out of the dark mine of that personality precious jewels for our Lord. Perhaps we are terribly tempted to despair, because of continual disappointments and what seems like hopeless weakness of character. But we are not alone. The search, the long effort, is lighted by the presence of our God. He is not baffled by personality. His promises are light. So let us go on, despairing of no man, for the jewel mine is His. He died to purchase it. *Behold, all souls are Mine* is His word (Ezekiel 18:4).[2]

AMY CARMICHAEL IN WHISPERS OF HIS POWER

Believe God's word and power more than you believe your own feelings and experiences. Your Rock is Christ, and it is not the Rock which ebbs and flows, but your sea. *(Samuel Rutherford)*

Keep your eyes steadily fixed on the infinite grandeur of Christ's finished work and righteousness. Look to Jesus and believe, look to Jesus and live! Nay, more; as you look to him, hoist your sails and buffet manfully the sea of life. Do not remain in the haven of distrust, or sleeping on your shadows in inactive repose, or suffering your frames and feelings to pitch and toss on one another like vessels idly moored in a harbor. The religious life is not a brooding over emotions, grazing the keel of faith in the shallows, or dragging the anchor of hope through the oozy tide of mud as if afraid of encountering the healthy breeze. Away! With your canvas spread to the gale, trusting in Him, who rules the raging of the waters. The safety of the tinted bird is to be on the wing. If its haunt be near the ground—if it fly low—it exposes itself to the fowler's net or snare. If we remain groveling on the low ground of feeling and emotion, we shall find ourselves entangled in a thousand meshes of doubt and despondency, temptation and unbelief.[3]

MRS. CHARLES COWMAN IN STREAMS IN THE DESERT

ENJOY HIS PRESENCE

How has God shown you His perspective in recent days? In what way do you need His discerning heart today?

REST IN HIS LOVE

> "Whoever is wise, let him understand these things;
> Whoever is discerning, let him know them.
> For the ways of the LORD are right,
> And the righteous will walk in them,
> But transgressors will stumble in them." (Hosea 14:9)

the passionate heart

How can I give you up, O Ephraim?
How can I surrender you, O Israel . . .
My heart is turned over within Me,
All My compassions are kindled.

HOSEA 11:8

Prepare Your Heart

As you continue your journey to God's heart, you will share His passion for people. You will dream His dreams and be filled with His desires. You will experience an intense love for others and an enthusiasm to share God's truth from His Word. The only explanation for this passion that develops within you is that it is from God Himself.

Billy Sunday was known for just such a passion. His father died within a month of his birth in 1862. His mother, overwhelmed by the responsibility of raising children alone, sent both of her young boys to an orphanage. As a result, Sunday never knew his parents. At the age of twenty-one, he became a professional baseball player, joining the Chicago White Stockings. He gave his life to Christ in 1886 at the Pacific Garden Mission in Chicago. That decision changed the course of his life and the lives of millions of other people throughout the world.

How many lives are affected by the decision of one person for Christ! It is like a stone that falls into a lake. The ripples extend for thousands of miles and across generations. As a professional baseball player, Sunday was offered four hundred dollars a month, and later two thousand dollars a month—a fortune in those days. He turned it all down and decided to become a missionary worker at the YMCA for eighty-three dollars a month. Sunday gave his first revival sermon in 1897 and was ordained a minister in 1903. He was known as a fiery evangelist who inspired millions with his intense words, theatrics, and humor.

God raised Sunday up during a time when the United States was in a period of great growth and transition to a more urban, industrialized society. It is estimated that he preached to over one hundred million people. Perhaps as many as one million people came to Christ as a result of his passionate message of truth from the Word of God. He was radical in his time. God was pleased to use this common man in a phenomenal way, because that is what God loves to do in accomplishing His purposes. Billy Sunday was willing to share the passionate heart of God for His people and to live it out so that God could touch millions.

Intimacy with God produces astounding results that will extend far beyond your imagination. This same passion has driven so many down through the years to share Christ and His gospel with others. The list goes on and on: D. L. Moody, C. T. Studd, Gypsy Smith, Hannah Whitall Smith, Amy Carmichael, Billy Graham, Dawson Trotman, Henrietta Mears, and Bill Bright. There are others, unknown to us, who shared God's passionate heart and whose names are famous with Him. When they look into His face in eternity, they will have intimate knowledge of the experiences they shared with God during their brief stay on earth. Will you be one of those who shares God's heart in this way?

We see God's passionate heart in Hosea as God cries out, "How can I give you up, O Ephraim? How can I surrender you, O Israel? . . . My heart is turned over within Me, all My compassions are kindled" (Hosea 11:8). God's grace drives Him to reach out to people who turn their backs on Him. He never gives up, and He continues to initiate a relationship. The more you share in God's passionate heart, the more you will be moved to share Him with those around you. It will truly be, as the hymn says, your "theme in glory."

As you begin your quiet time today, meditate on the words of this great hymn, "I Love to Tell the Story," by Katherine Sankey.

> I love to tell the story
> of unseen things above,
> of Jesus and his glory,
> of Jesus and his love.
> I love to tell the story,
> because I know 'tis true;
> it satisfies my longings
> as nothing else can do.
>
> Refrain:
> I love to tell the story,
> 'twill be my theme in glory,
> to tell the old, old story
> of Jesus and his love.
>
> I love to tell the story;
> more wonderful it seems
> than all the golden fancies

of all our golden dreams.
I love to tell the story,
it did so much for me;
and that is just the reason
I tell it now to thee.

Refrain

I love to tell the story;
'tis pleasant to repeat
what seems, each time I tell it,
more wonderfully sweet.
I love to tell the story,
for some have never heard
the message of salvation
from God's own holy Word.

Refrain

I love to tell the story,
for those who know it best
seem hungering and thirsting
to hear it like the rest.
And when, in scenes of glory,
I sing the new, new song,
'twill be the old, old story
that I have loved so long.

Refrain

READ AND STUDY GOD'S WORD

Sharing God's passion for His people is the height of intimacy in the journey to His heart. It is what drives others to go beyond their own capabilities and rest in the adequacy of God.

1. Read Hosea 11, looking for God's passionate heart. What does God say that shows His passion for His people?

2. Hosea shared in God's passion for His people. Read Hosea 6 and record what Hosea said that reveals a passionate heart for God.

3. Look at the following statements by others throughout Scripture. How do you see this same passionate heart?
    Matthew 23:37 (Jesus speaking)

    Luke 23:33-34

    Acts 2:22-24,38-41 (Peter speaking)

    Romans 9:1-5; 10:1

    1 Corinthians 9:19-27

4. Summarize what you have learned about God's passion for His people.

5. In what ways are you sharing in God's heart for His people?

Adore God in Prayer

Take some time today and pray for those in your life who need to know Jesus. You may want to write their names on your Prayer Pages. Place each one before the throne of God, and know that the Lord whose eye sees the sparrow is also at work in your life and in the lives of those around you.

Yield Yourself to God

What must I do? Philosophy doesn't answer it. Infidelity doesn't answer it. First, *believe on the Lord Jesus Christ and thou shalt be saved.* Believe on the Lord. Lord—that's His kingly name. That's the name he reigns under. *Thou shalt call His name Jesus.* It takes that kind of a confession. Give me a Savior with a sympathetic eye to watch me so I shall not slander. Give me a Savior with a strong arm to catch me if I stumble. Give me a Savior that will hear my slightest moan. Believe on the Lord Jesus Christ and be saved. Christ is His resurrection name. He is sitting at the right hand of the Father interceding for us.

Because of his divinity he understands God's side of it and because of his humanity he understands our side of it. Who is better qualified to be a mediator? He's a mediator. What is that? A lawyer is a mediator between the jury and the defendant. A retail merchant is a mediator between the wholesale dealer and the consumer. Therefore, Jesus Christ is the mediator between God and man. Believe on the Lord. He's ruling today. Believe on the Lord Jesus. He died to save us. Believe on the Lord Jesus Christ. He's the Mediator.

Her Majesty, Queen Victoria, was traveling in Scotland when a storm came up and she took refuge in a little hut of a Highlander. She stayed there for an hour and when she went, the good wife said to her husband, "We'll tie a ribbon on that chair because her majesty has sat on it and no one else will ever sit on it." A friend of mine was there later and was going to sit in the chair when the man cried: "Nae, nae, mon. Dinna sit there. Her majesty spent an hour with us once and she sat on that chair and we tied a ribbon on it and no one else will ever sit on it." They were honored that her majesty had spent the hour with them. It brought unspeakable joy to them.

It's great that Jesus Christ will sit on the throne of my heart, not for an hour, but here to sway his power forever and ever.[1]

FROM A SERMON BY BILLY SUNDAY IN BILLY SUNDAY, THE MAN AND HIS MESSAGE

ENJOY HIS PRESENCE

As you think about your own life, whose passion for Christ and sharing of the gospel has influenced you the most? What qualities were apparent in that person's life?

REST IN HIS LOVE

"Brethren, my heart's desire and my prayer to God for them is for their salvation" (Romans 10:1).

DEAR FRIEND,

The next two days are your opportunity to spend time reviewing what you have learned this week. You may wish to write your thoughts and insights in your Journal. As you think about all you have learned about the journey to the heart of God, record:

Your most significant insight:

Your favorite quote:

Your favorite verse:

Where are you in this journey to the heart of God? In what ways are you sharing God's heart?

As you read the following poem, think about how God has chosen you as His beloved and desires you to dance day by day with Him. As you read, talk with the Lord about the truths you have learned from His Word this week. Share with Him all that is on your heart.

Roadmates

Come, share the road with Me, My own,
Through good and evil weather;
Two better speed than one alone,
So let us go together.

Come, share the road with Me, My own,
You know I'll never fail you,
And doubts and fears of the unknown
Shall never more assail you.

Come, share the road with Me, My own,
I'll share your joys and sorrows.
And hand in hand we'll seek the throne
And God's great glad tomorrows.

Come, share the road with Me, My own,
And where the black clouds gather,
I'll share thy load with thee, My son,
And we'll press on together.

And as we go, we'll share also
With all who travel on it.
For all who share the road with Me
Must share with all upon it.

So make we—all one company,
Love's golden cord our tether,
And, come what may, we'll climb the way
Together—aye, together![1]

JOHN OXENHAM

face to face with God

week
three

MOSES

face to face as a friend

Thus the LORD used to speak to Moses face to face,
just as a man speaks to his friend.
EXODUS 33:11

Prepare Your Heart

In 1930 a group of gifted men began meeting weekly. They called themselves the Inklings. The core group of the Inklings included C. S. Lewis, J. R. R. Tolkien, and Charles Williams. They became close friends as a result of their time together. During their celebrated gatherings in Lewis's rooms at Magdalen College at Oxford, they talked, shared a beverage, and read their latest projects to the group. Then they would discuss the works together.

The exchange of ideas influenced their writings. Well-known projects such as Lewis's *The Screwtape Letters* and Tolkien's *The Lord of the Rings* enjoyed the scholarly scrutiny and critique of the Inklings. This same group also met on Tuesday mornings at an English pub called The Eagle and Child, affectionately nicknamed by them The Bird and Baby. Other writers and scholars would often join in the lively sessions, where thoughts and ideas were freely shared. Lewis once said of this group, "What I owe to them is incalculable." It is easy to imagine how exciting it must have been for those brilliant scholars and writers to exchange ideas in the context of a friendship that was nurtured through much time together.

In the same way, God desires to grow an intimate friendship with you. What does that mean? This week you will look at one man who had such a relationship. Moses met God one day on a mountain. Thus began a famous relationship between an extraordinary God and an ordinary man who turned aside to see why a bush was burning on its own in the desert. That day, God spoke for the first time to Moses. It was the first of many lively exchanges between the two.

How did they spend time together? In Exodus 33:11 we learn something very important about the kind of intimate relationship we can have with God. We are told, "The LORD used to speak to Moses face to face, just as a man speaks to his friend." Try to wrap your mind around what this could possibly mean. We know that no man can see the face of God and live (see Exodus 33:20). What then does "face to face" mean? It means heart to heart, person to person. No masks. You expose to God the *you* that can be touched and moved and changed.

Just as the Inklings influenced each other by spending lively times together, so you are influenced by the exchange between you and God. To speak "face to face, just as a man speaks to his friend" means to *keep company with God*. It means that you are an intimate of God. It means you have a great thing going with God. You look forward to your times together. You share your deepest thoughts with Him. And you cannot wait to tell God everything on your heart. That is the way it was with Moses and God. This week you will see it. But your real goal is to know it for yourself in your own life. Then your heart will dance with the Lord.

As you prepare for your time with the Lord today, ask Him to give you a face-to-face relationship with Him, "just as a man speaks to his friend." You may wish to write a prayer to the Lord expressing what is on your heart.

READ AND STUDY GOD'S WORD

Today you want to gain a deeper understanding of the kind of relationship Moses had with the Lord. Remember, to be intimate does not mean to shelve your brain. The opposite is true. You engage in the deepest of thought as you converse with Him. Moses was an intimate of God. He walked with God. He kept company with God. This is really a description and definition of prayer. Is not prayer simply the intimate conversation that takes place in the context of your relationship with God? It is not some mystical exercise that occurs only on the highest mountains. Your goal is to learn how to keep company with God as Moses did: Person to person, Heart to heart.

  1. Turn to Exodus 33:7-11 and record everything you learn about Moses and his relationship with God. As you write your insights, use as many of the actual phrases from Scripture as possible.

2. According to the superscription, Moses wrote Psalm 90. Read this psalm. What is your favorite phrase?

v12 teach us to make the most of our time, so that we may grow in wisdom.

3. Read Psalm 90 again and record all that Moses had learned about God.

he sees all our sins
he has been our home
he is powerful & gets very angry
he has unfailing love

4. Read the psalm again and write out those things that Moses desired from God. What request is the desire of your heart today?

5. In light of what you have read in Psalm 90, how would you describe the view Moses had of God?

He praises God as our King

ADORE GOD IN PRAYER

Rosalind Rinker described a defining moment in her life when she discovered with another friend the true nature of prayer—that it is *conversing with God*. She said, "Do you know what? I believe the Lord taught us something just now! Instead of each of us making a prayer-speech to Him, let's talk things over with Him, back and forth, including Him in it, as we do when we have a conversation."[1]

Take some time now to talk things over with God. What is on your heart? Talk with Him about it. Think about what you have heard Him say in His Word today. Be still and hear Him speak in His Word. Converse with Him from your heart as you would with a friend.

YIELD YOURSELF TO GOD

It is an incontrovertible fact that some Christians seem to experience a much closer intimacy with God than others. They appear to enjoy a reverent familiarity with Him that is foreign to us. Is it a matter of favoritism or caprice on the part of God? Or do such people qualify in some way for that desirable intimacy? . . . Both Scripture and experience teach that it is we, not God, who determine the degree of intimacy with Him that we enjoy. We are at this moment as close to God as we really choose to be. True, there are times when we would like to know a deeper intimacy, but when it comes to the point, we are not prepared to pay the price involved. The qualifying conditions are more stringent and exacting than we are prepared to meet; so we settle for a less demanding level of Christian living. Everything in our Christian life and service flows from our relationship with God. If we are not in vital fellowship with Him, everything else will be out of focus. But when our communion with Him is close and real, it is gloriously possible to experience a growing intimacy.[2]

J. OSWALD SANDERS IN *ENJOYING INTIMACY WITH GOD*

After years of feeling useless and guilty, I began to realize the truth of a comment made by one of the early Fathers of the church, Clement of Alexandria. He said that *prayer is keeping company with God*. This began to give me a new focus on prayer. I began to see prayer more as a friendship than a rigorous discipline. It started to become more of a relationship and less of a performance.[3]

JAMES HOUSTON IN *THE TRANSFORMING POWER OF PRAYER: DEEPENING YOUR FRIENDSHIP WITH GOD*

Wherever faith has been original, wherever it has proved itself to be real, it has invariably had upon it a sense of the *present* God. The holy Scriptures possess in marked degree this feeling of actual encounter with a real Person. The men and women of the Bible talked with God. They spoke to Him and heard Him speak in words they could understand. With Him they held person to person converse, and a sense of shining reality is upon their words and deeds. . . . But better far is the sense of *Someone there*. It was this that filled with abiding wonder the first members of the Church of Christ. The solemn delight which those early disciples knew sprang straight from the conviction that there was One in the midst of them. They knew that the Majesty in the heavens was confronting them on earth: they were in the very Presence of God. And the power of that conviction to arrest attention and hold it for a lifetime, to elevate, to transform, to fill with uncontrollable moral happiness, to send men singing to prison and to death, has been one of the wonders of history and a marvel of the world.[4]

A. W. TOZER IN *THE DIVINE CONQUEST*

ENJOY HIS PRESENCE

What have you learned today that you will carry with you throughout the day? Write down your thoughts.

REST IN HIS LOVE

"Just as I have been with Moses, I will be with you; I will not fail you or forsake you" (God's words to Joshua in Joshua 1:5).

turn aside to look

So Moses said, "I must turn aside now and see this marvelous sight,
why the bush is not burned up."
EXODUS 3:3

Prepare Your Heart

In C. S. Lewis's *Chronicles of Narnia*, the adventures begin with a huge piece of furniture called a wardrobe. It is ornate, mysterious, and inviting. It is so inviting that a young girl named Lucy, while playing hide and seek, cannot resist the temptation to step inside and discover its contents. The wardrobe is just a piece of furniture, but when she ventures inside, Lucy finds another world, one entirely different from what she knows.

Moses grew up amid the wealth of Egypt. He saw the finer things in life. He lived in the busyness of a moving, growing culture. But after committing a crime, he had to flee from his familiar life. He traveled through the wilderness and settled in faraway Midian. He married Zipporah and made a life in the desert. He was in charge of a flock of sheep owned by Jethro, his father-in-law.

One day, Moses was alone in the wilderness as he led his flock to Mount Horeb. What happened that day changed everything. But nothing would have happened had Moses not *turned aside to look.*

Here is the question for you today: Have you learned how to—moment by moment—throughout the day, turn aside to look, so that you might see and hear from God? If you will turn aside to look, you will begin to notice that God is there. You will take part in that great adventure of knowing God and enjoying intimacy with Him. Moment by moment, you will enter into His world and experience Him in this life.

Turn to Psalm 33 and read the words slowly, phrase by phrase. What phrase is most significant to you today?

v 22 Let your unfailing love surround us, Lord for our hope is in you alone.

READ AND STUDY GOD'S WORD

1. Today you will look at the first meeting between Moses and God. What an event that must have been! And what a blessing it is that Moses wrote it down so that you could know what it was like to meet God for the first time. Read Exodus 3:1-6. What is most significant to you about this first encounter between God and Moses?

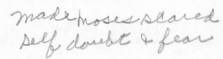

that he wasn't afraid, he was very obedient

2. Read Exodus 3:7–4:18. Try to imagine yourself in the place of Moses, as though God were saying these things to you. How do you think this first meeting with God affected Moses? How do you think it made a difference in his life?

made moses scared self doubt & fear

3. Look at the following verses and record what you learn about how the presence of God makes a difference in your everyday life. How does intimacy with God influence your life? Personalize your answers.

Isaiah 41:10

Isaiah 43:1-2

Isaiah 54:10-17

Romans 8:37

Ephesians 1:18-19

4. How does God's presence in your everyday life make a difference?

ADORE GOD IN PRAYER

By day and by night,
in life and in death,
may I ever be true to you,
O Lover of my soul,
My ceaseless Friend,
My unchangeable Savior.
Into your hands
I commit my soul.[1]

F. B. MEYER IN *DAILY PRAYERS*

YIELD YOURSELF TO GOD

There were no hints, no premonitions, no special signs to alert [Moses] to the fact that God Himself would break the silence that day and that life would change forever. It was just your common, ordinary, garden-variety day-shift with the sheep. Nothing more. Nothing less. Nothing else. Just another day at the wilderness office, under the shadow of Mount Horeb. The sun came up, the sheep grazed, and Moses chalked off his 14,600th day as Jethro's assistant shepherd. That is the way God works. Without even a hint of warning, He speaks to ordinary people, on ordinary days. . . . I'm not saying that every *coincidence* is God's burning bush in your life. But I am saying this: God may use an extraordinary event or circumstance to tap you on the shoulder, in order to grab your undivided attention. He may use something like that to intrude into your daily life and say, *Wait a minute. Stop. Be still. I have something to say to you.* When you and I come across extremely unusual events, it's a good idea to ask, *Could God be saying something to me now?*[2]

CHARLES SWINDOLL IN *MOSES*

This incident brings to our minds the fact that there are two kinds of knowledge. There is a knowledge that comes from description. One person describes a thing to another, and the other person gains some knowledge of it. We can give knowledge to others by description.

Then there is the knowledge that comes from experience. It is possible to describe a battle fought in a war. But the soldier who has gone through the hell of actual shot and shell and fire knows the battle by personal experience. The memory is for a lifetime. It is something he cannot escape.

It was in this sense that Moses met God at the burning bush. He was a man experiencing the presence of God. To Moses, God was no longer an idea from history, but a living Person willing to become involved with His creation, mankind.[3]

A. W. Tozer in *Men Who Met God*

The spiritual giants of old were men who at some time became acutely conscious of the real Presence of God and maintained that consciousness for the rest of their lives. The first encounter may have been one of terror, as when a *horror of great darkness* fell upon Abram, or as when Moses at the bush hid his face because he was afraid to look upon God. Usually this fear soon lost its content of terror and changed after a while to delightsome awe, to level off finally into a reverent sense of complete nearness to God. The essential point is, *they experienced God*. How otherwise can the saints and prophets be explained? How otherwise can we account for the amazing power for good they have exercised over countless generations? Is it not that they walked in conscious communion with the real Presence and addressed their prayers to God with the artless conviction that they were addressing Someone actually there?[4]

A. W. Tozer in *The Divine Conquest*

Enjoy His Presence

Are you acutely aware, as Tozer said, that God is with you? Think about this today, and look for Him as you go about your day. Take time to turn aside and look as you walk with Him. Take note of how He is working in and through you.

Rest in His Love

"I am with you always, even to the end of the age" (Jesus in Matthew 28:20).

remove your shoes

"Remove your sandals from your feet, for the place on
which you are standing is holy ground."
Exodus 3:5

Prepare Your Heart

What does it take to know God, to be intimate with Him? First and foremost, it requires humility. In Numbers 12:3 Moses is described as "very humble, more than any man who was on the face of the earth." Moses alone entered the Tent of Meeting to speak face to face with God. It is no coincidence that the most humble man was given the greatest intimacy with God.

Humility is a requirement to be intimate with God. His greatness can be seen only by those who have none of their own. The less you see of yourself, the more you will see of God. It does not mean that you are not talented. It may be, in fact, that you are brilliant. What it does mean is that you are far more interested in looking at God than at yourself. That is a sign of true humility.

Today your goal is to understand what it means to walk in humility before a holy God. Remove your shoes, and walk barefoot before God, for wherever God is, you are on holy ground.

Meditate on the words of Psalm 113 as a preparation for your time with the Lord today. After you have read it through once, pray this psalm to the Lord, personalizing it and directing it to Him. For example, "I praise You, O Lord. . . . Blessed be your name from this time forth and forever."

READ AND STUDY GOD'S WORD

1. Today you will look again at the first meeting between God and Moses. Turn to Exodus 3:1-6. Why do you think God asked Moses to remove his sandals from his feet?

to humble himself befor God.

What does it mean to be humble? It means to make a true estimate of ourselves in the presence of our majestic and holy God. It involves a sense of complete dependence on God because we realize our inadequacy and weakness apart from Him. Andrew Murray said humility is "our participation in the life of Jesus."[1] Jesus was, according to Matthew 11:29, "gentle and humble in heart." He came to do the Father's will. That is the act of a humble person. The humble one never exalts self, but only God and His desires.

2. Look at the following passages and record what you learn about humility. What humbles a person? Take time especially with Deuteronomy 8, noting the value of humility in the lives of the Israelites.

Deuteronomy 8

2 Chronicles 7:14

Psalm 25:9

Proverbs 11:2

1 Peter 5:5-7

3. How would you define humility? What do you think God desires when He asks you to be humble?

to put God first
to lower your pride

4. How does humility help you become intimate with God?

He realizes

ADORE GOD IN PRAYER
As you worship God in prayer today and talk to Him, you might pray the words of this hymn written by Charles Wesley (1707–1788). If you know the melody, you may wish to sing it to the Lord.

> Love divine, all loves excelling,
> joy of heaven, to earth come down;
> fix in us thy humble dwelling;
> all thy faithful mercies crown!
> Jesus thou art all compassion,
> pure, unbounded love thou art;
> visit us with thy salvation;
> enter every trembling heart.
>
> Breathe, O breathe thy loving Spirit
> into every troubled breast!
> Let us all in thee inherit;
> let us find that second rest.
> Take away our bent to sinning;
> Alpha and Omega be;
> end of faith, as its beginning,
> set our hearts at liberty.
>
> Come, Almighty to deliver,
> let us all thy life receive;
> suddenly return and never,
> nevermore thy temples leave.
> Thee we would be always blessing,

serve thee as thy hosts above,
pray and praise thee without ceasing,
glory in thy perfect love.

Finish, then, thy new creation;
pure and spotless let us be.
Let us see thy great salvation
perfectly restored in thee;
changed from glory into glory,
till in heaven we take our place,
till we cast our crowns before thee,
lost in wonder, love, and praise.

YIELD YOURSELF TO GOD

The presence of God demanded a holistic preparation of the one who would aspire to enter his presence. Therefore, to teach Moses this lesson, God set up admittedly arbitrary boundaries—*do not come any closer*—and commanded that he should also remove his sandals. This was to prevent him from rashly intruding into the presence of God and to teach him that God was separate and distinct from mortal men. Because God was present, what had been ordinary became *holy ground* and consequently *set apart* for a distinct use.[2]

WALTER C. KAISER JR. IN *EXPOSITOR'S BIBLE COMMENTARY*

We must learn of Jesus, how He is meek and lowly of heart. He teaches us where true humility takes its rise and finds its strength: in the knowledge that it is God who worketh all in all, and that our place is to yield to Him in perfect resignation and dependence—in full consent to be and to do nothing of ourselves. This is the life Christ came to reveal and to impart—a life to God that came through death to sin and self. If we feel that this life is too high for us and beyond our reach, this insight must but the more urge us to seek it in Him—for it is the indwelling Christ who will live in us this life, meek and lowly. If we long for this, let us, meanwhile, above everything, seek the holy secret of the knowledge of the nature of God, as He every moment works all in all—the secret, of which all nature and every creature, and above all, every child of God, is to be the witness: that it is nothing but a vessel, a channel, through which the living God can manifest the riches of His wisdom, power, and goodness. The root of all virtue and grace, of all faith and acceptable worship, is that we know that we have nothing but what we receive, and bow in deepest humility to wait upon God for it.[3]

ANDREW MURRAY IN *HUMILITY*

ENJOY HIS PRESENCE

As you close your time today, write a prayer to the Lord in your Journal, thanking Him for what He has shown you in your time with Him. Ask Him to show you how you can walk through life—with shoes removed, so to speak—in awe and reverence, worshiping and honoring Him throughout the day.

REST IN HIS LOVE

"For this is what the high and lofty One says—he who lives forever, whose name is holy: 'I live in a high and holy place, but also with him who is contrite and lowly in spirit, to revive the spirit of the lowly and to revive the heart of the contrite'" (Isaiah 57:15, NIV).

extravagantly desire God

Then Moses said, "I pray You, show me Your glory!"
EXODUS 33:18

Prepare Your Heart

A. W. Tozer was a master of worship and a deep thinker. One biographer describes him as a student in the school of Jesus.[1] The Bible was his textbook. Warren Wiersbe said that Tozer "begs us to please God and forget the crowd. He implores us to worship God that we might become more like Him."[2]

Tozer grew up on a farm and became a Christian at eighteen. Once he came to Christ, he was a different person. The Lord awakened his intellect and filled him with a sense of purpose. He was intense in his love for the Lord. He would often withdraw from others to find a quiet place for Bible study, prayer, and communion with God. He would keep a small notebook to record requests for himself and others. At the outset of his ministry he prayed a prayer of commitment to the Lord and later wrote out the prayer. Near the end of it, he said:

And now, O Lord of heaven and earth, I consecrate my remaining days to Thee; let them be many or few, as Thou wilt. Let me stand before the great or minister to the poor and lowly; that choice is not mine, and I would not influence it if I could. I am Thy servant to do Thy will, and that will is sweeter to me than position or riches or fame, and I choose it above all things on earth or in heaven.

Though I am chosen of Thee and honored by a high and holy calling, let me never forget that I am but a man of dust and ashes, a man with all the natural faults and passions that plague the race of men. I pray Thee, therefore, my Lord and Redeemer, save me from myself and from all the injuries I may do myself while trying to be a blessing to others. Fill me with Thy power by the Holy Spirit, and I will go in Thy strength and tell of Thy righteousness, even Thine only. I will spread abroad the message of redeeming love while my normal powers endure. Then, dear Lord, when I am old and weary and too tired to go on, have a place ready for me above, and make me to be numbered with Thy saints in glory everlasting. *Amen.*[3]

Is that prayer yours today? Do you desire God above anything else? Ask God today to fill your heart with a passionate love and desire for Him. You may wish to write a prayer as you begin your time alone with Him.

READ AND STUDY GOD'S WORD

1. Moses was the most humble man in the world. But he also made the most extravagant requests of God. Humility does not mean lack of desire when it comes to God. If anything, the humble man or woman will press for the most from the Lord. You may be bold with Him, even extravagant. Oh, how the Lord loves it when one of His children runs into the throne room and asks to see Him as He really is! That is what Moses did one day. Read Exodus 33 and record what Moses asked of God.

2. What do you think was Moses' most extravagant request?

3. How did God respond to Moses' requests?

4. In what ways are you extravagant in your pursuit to know God and in your conversations with Him?

ADORE GOD IN PRAYER

Use these words of Amy Carmichael as a prayer to the Lord today.

> *I could not see*
> *For the glory of that light.*
> Let the shining of that glory
> Illumine our sight.
>
> Things temporal
> Are transparent in that air.
> But the things that are eternal
> Are manifest there.
>
> Jesus our Lord,
> By the virtue of Thy grace,
> In the shining of Thy glory
> Let us see Thy face.[4]

YIELD YOURSELF TO GOD

The man of God! How much that name means! A man who comes from God, chosen and sent by Him. One who walks with God, lives in His fellowship, and carries the mark of His presence. A man who lives for God and His will; whose whole being is pervaded and ruled by the glory of God; who unknowingly and unceasingly leads others to think of God. A man in whose heart and life God has taken the right place as the All in All, and a man who has only one desire, that God should have His rightful place throughout the world. Such men of God are what the world needs; God seeks them, that He may fill them with Himself, and send them into the world to help others to know Him. Moses was so obviously such a man that people naturally spoke of him thus—Moses the man of God! Every servant of God ought to aim at being such a person—a living witness and proof of what God is to him in heaven and on earth, and what He claims to be in all people.[5]

ANDREW MURRAY IN *THE INNER LIFE*

Come near to the holy men and women of the past and you will soon feel the heat of their desire after God. They mourned for Him, they prayed and wrestled and sought for Him day and night, in season and out, and when they had found Him the finding was all the sweeter for the long seeking. Moses used the fact that he knew God as an argument for knowing Him better. *Now, therefore, I pray thee, if I have found grace in thy sight, show me now thy way, that I may know thee, that I may find grace in thy sight;* and from there he rose to make the daring request, *I beseech thee, show me thy glory.* God was frankly pleased by this display of ardor, and the next day called Moses into the mount, and there in solemn procession made all His glory pass before him.[6]

A. W. TOZER IN THE PURSUIT OF GOD

ENJOY HIS PRESENCE

How has God spoken to you today? What are the great desires in your life? Do they include the Lord, your God? Write your thoughts. Then, close your time thanking the Lord for all that He has shown you. Pray the extravagant prayers of Moses throughout the day today.

Meditate on the words of this hymn by Fanny Crosby:

> A wonderful Savior is Jesus my Lord,
> A wonderful Savior to me;
> He hideth my soul in the cleft of the rock,
> Where rivers of pleasure I see.
>
> Refrain:
> He hideth my soul in the cleft of the rock
> That shadows a dry, thirsty land;
> He hideth my life with the depths of His love,
> And covers me there with His hand,
> And covers me there with His hand.
>
> A wonderful Savior is Jesus my Lord,
> He taketh my burden away;
> He holdeth me up, and I shall not be moved,
> He giveth me strength as my day.
>
> Refrain
>
> With numberless blessings each moment He crowns,
> And filled with His fullness divine,
> I sing in my rapture, oh, glory to God
> For such a Redeemer as mine!
>
> Refrain

When clothed in His brightness, transported I rise
To meet Him in clouds of the sky,
His perfect salvation, His wonderful love
I'll shout with the millions on high.

Refrain

REST IN HIS LOVE

"For God, who said, 'Light shall shine out of darkness,' is the One who has shone in our hearts to give the Light of the knowledge of the glory of God in the face of Christ" (2 Corinthians 4:6).

climb the mountain

Moses rose up early in the morning and went up to Mount Sinai,
as the LORD had commanded him.

EXODUS 34:4

Prepare Your Heart

Oswald Chambers is a man of God who will help you think deliberately about your Lord. He can help you come to an unwavering commitment that leads you further on the path to intimacy with God. His words are filled with conviction, especially those in his classic *My Utmost for His Highest*. Chambers was a scholar, and he loved God above all. One author describes him as "an unbribed soul." He spoke the truth in plain language that leads you to the Lord and His Word. He told his students to "ransack their Bibles."[1]

Oswald Chambers loved and often quoted these words:

Christ! I am Christ's! and let the name suffice you,
Ay, for me too He greatly hath sufficed;
Lo with no winning words I would entice you,
Paul has no honour and no friend but Christ.

Yea, thro' life, death, thro' sorrow and thro' sinning
He shall suffice me, for He hath sufficed:
Christ is the end, for Christ was the beginning,
Christ the beginning, for the end is Christ.[2]

This week we have been looking at Moses' intimate friendship with God, face to face, speaking as a man would to a friend. Many of the meetings between Moses and God took place on Mount Sinai. After Moses' extravagant request to see God's glory, God told him to present himself on the top of the mountain.

The Lord invites you to take the journey up Mount Sinai to meet with Him. Whenever you turn aside to look at Him and spend time with Him, it involves a climb. It can mean getting up early just like Moses, preparing, and going off to meet with your Lord. It may at times fatigue you. But the view is worth the climb.

As you begin your quiet time with the Lord, ask Him to quiet your heart and prepare you to meet with Him.

READ AND STUDY GOD'S WORD

1. Yesterday, in reading Exodus 33, you had the opportunity to read about the extravagant desire of Moses to see his God. Today you are going to look at how God met him on the mountain. Read Exodus 34:1-11 and describe what happened on the mountain. What did Moses see? And how did he respond?

2. In what way did meeting with God that morning involve preparation? In what way does your meeting with God each day involve preparation?

3. It is important for you to know that you can have the same kind of intimacy with God that Moses experienced. It is there for you if only you will meet with God "on the mountain," so to speak. Turn to 2 Corinthians 3:2-18 and record your insights about how our experience with God compares and contrasts with that of Moses.

ADORE GOD IN PRAYER

Turn to your Prayer Pages today and record as requests to the Lord those things that are weighing on your heart. Take them to Him today and talk to Him about each burden. Go to the mountain and keep company with Him, speaking with Him face to face, person to person, heart to heart.

YIELD YOURSELF TO GOD

The battle is lost or won in the secret places of the will before God, never first in the external world. The Spirit of God apprehends me and I am obliged to get alone with God and fight the battle out before Him. Until this is done, I lose every time. The battle may take one minute or a year, that will depend on me, not on God, and I must resolutely go through the hell of a renunciation before God. Nothing has any power over the man who has fought out the battle before God and won there. If I say, *I will wait till I get into the circumstances and then put God to the test*, I shall find I cannot. I must get the thing settled between myself and God in the secret places of my soul where no stranger intermeddles, and then I can go forth with the certainty that the battle is won. . . . Get alone with God, fight it out before Him, settle the matter there once and for all. . . . Every now and again, not often, God brings us to a point of climax. That is the Great Divide in the life; from that point we either go towards a more and more dilatory and useless type of Christian life, or we become more and more ablaze for the glory of God—My Utmost For His Highest.[3]

OSWALD CHAMBERS IN *MY UTMOST FOR HIS HIGHEST*

May not the inadequacy of much of our spiritual experience be traced back to our habit of skipping through the corridors of the Kingdom like children through the market place, chattering about everything, but pausing to learn the true value of nothing? In my creature impatience I am often caused to wish that there were some way to bring modern Christians into a deeper spiritual life painlessly by short easy lessons; but such wishes are vain. No short cut exists. God has not bowed to our nervous haste nor embraced the methods of our machine age. It is well that we accept the hard truth now: *the man who would know God must give time to Him*. He must count no time wasted which is spent in the cultivation of His acquaintance. He must give himself to meditation and prayer hours on end. So did the saints of old, the glorious company of the apostles, the goodly fellowship of the prophets and the believing members of the holy Church in all generations. And so must we if we would follow in their train.[4]

A. W. TOZER IN *THE DIVINE CONQUEST*

Enjoy His Presence

What was your most significant insight today as you spent time with the Lord? How will you apply it to your life today? Record your thoughts. Then close by thanking the Lord for what He has shown you.

Rest in His Love

"In the early morning, while it was still dark, Jesus got up, left the house, and went away to a secluded place, and was praying there" (Mark 1:35).

DEAR FRIEND,

The next two days are your opportunity to spend time reviewing what you have learned this week. You may wish to write your thoughts and insights in your Journal. As you think about all you have learned about having a relationship that is face to face with God, record:

Your most significant insight:

Your favorite quote:

Your favorite verse:

How do you think the intimate friendship between God and Moses influenced Moses' life?

How has knowing God influenced your life?

Close this week by meditating on the following words:

It would seem that admission to the inner circle of deepening intimacy with God is the outcome of *deep desire*. Only those who count such intimacy a prize worth sacrificing anything else for are likely to attain it.[1]

J. Oswald Sanders in Enjoying Intimacy with God

God is looking for a man, or woman, whose heart will be always set on Him, and who will trust Him for all He desires to do. God is eager to work more mightily now than He ever has through any soul. The clock of the centuries points to the eleventh hour. *The world is waiting yet to see what God can do through a consecrated soul.* Not the world alone, but God Himself is waiting for one, who will be more fully devoted to Him than any who have ever lived; who will be willing to be nothing that Christ may be all; who will grasp God's own purposes; and taking His humility and His faith, His love and His power, will, without hindering, continue to let God do exploits.[2]

C. H. P., as told by Mrs. Charles Cowman in Streams in the Desert

a heart that dances

week
four

DAVID

chasing after His will

"I have found David the son of Jesse, a man after My heart, who will do all My will."
ACTS 13:22

Prepare Your Heart

Every now and then, certain people stand out in the crowd. They stand out, not because of what they possess or the power they have, but because they are of a different breed. There is something about the way they move and the look in their eyes. There is a determination, an energy, and an extraordinary love that seems to know no end in their life. It touches everything and everyone around them. In their eyes you can see all the way to the heart. What do you see there? A heart that dances. It dances in perfect step with the Lord Jesus Christ. There may be a few wrong moves, but the adjustment is quick and the movement fluid and effortless.

David was such a man. God said this about David: "I have found David the son of Jesse, a man after My heart, who will do all My will" (Acts 13:22). That is the description of one who has a heart that dances. Such a one has a heart like the Lord's, keeps in step with Him, and chases after His will. There is no question of *if* he or she will ever carry out the Lord's desires. This heart runs toward the Lord, follows Him, and actively desires to please Him in every respect. It desires to delight the One it loves. The heart that dances rejoices in the Lover of his or her soul. No adversity can crush its joy. The presence of the Lord is enough to fulfill that heart for a lifetime.

This week you are going to look at David, the man after God's heart. Your goal is to discover the heart that dances and experience it for yourself.

As you begin your time with the Lord, turn to Psalm 26. What qualities do you see in this heart of David today? Record your insights. Then write a prayer in your Journal, pouring out those things that weigh heavily on you. Ask the Lord to speak to you today and to show you what it means to have that great heart He desires.

READ AND STUDY GOD'S WORD

1. David was the shepherd boy whom God chose to be king of His people, Israel. David is best seen in contrast to Saul, the first king of Israel. Turn to 1 Samuel 12 and record your insights about what God desires in the hearts of His people and their king.

God was to be their true King & they were subject to his laws.

2. Saul did not have the same heart as David. Read 1 Samuel 13 and 15. What do you learn about Saul and David, and about how God felt toward each of them?

Saul

Saul was more concerned about what others would think of him than he was about his relationship with God

David (1 Samuel 13:14; 15:28)

He was a man after his own heart

3. Read 1 Samuel 16:1-13. What do you learn about David, the one God chose to be king? Also, what do you see about how God chooses a person?

He was anointed king but it was done in secret - God judges by faith & character

4. God saw that David was one who would do all His will (see Acts 13:22). Look at the following verses. What do you learn about what it means to chase after God's will? Be sure to personalize your answers. For example, "I am to try to learn what is pleasing to the Lord."

Ephesians 5:1-10

Colossians 1:9-10

1 Thessalonians 4:1-8

Hebrews 13:18-21

1 John 3:22

Adore God in Prayer

O Holy Savior, make my life deeper, stronger, richer, gentler, more Christlike, more full of the spirit of heaven, more devoted to your service and glory, so that I may ever bless and praise you, and magnify your name and adorn your Gospel in all things.[1]

F. B. Meyer in *Daily Prayers*

Yield Yourself to God

"Thy kingdom come, Thy will be done. . . . " Aristotle once said, "Will moves through desire." The thought has merit. *Will* is a much stronger word than *purpose* or *intention*. When a bride tells the minister *I will!* in answer to his question, it carries an emphatic sound that *I intend* cannot match. Perhaps what she is saying, with all the urgency of her love, is *I desire!* Let's apply Aristotle's statement to the verse in the Lord's Prayer with which we began: *Your will be done.* We now read it as *Your desire be done.* Instead of engaging in endless theological and philosophical discussions as to the nature and interpretation of God's will, let us simply ask, *What is God's desire?*[2]

Sherwood E. Wirt in *Jesus Man of Joy*

You may not be intellectual or well thought of in your family circle; you may be despised by others for your faith in Christ. Perhaps you had only a little share in the love of your parents, as David did. But remember that those who are rejected of men often become beloved of the Lord. Your faith in the Lord Jesus may be very weak and you may realize little of the dignity which Christ has purposed for you, but the thought of God toward you began before He ever flung a star into space. Then He wrote your name on His heart; it was graven in the palms of His hand before the sky was stretched out in the heavens. You may consider yourself very obscure and unknown, just a unit in the mass, a cog in the machine. Like David, you might well say, *I was as a beast before Thee* (Psalm 73:22), and *I am a worm, and no man* (Psalm 22:6). Yet in His abundant mercy God can stoop down from heaven's highest glory to lift a beggar from the dunghill and set him among princes.[3]

ALAN REDPATH IN *THE MAKING OF A MAN OF GOD*

ENJOY HIS PRESENCE

Describe what you think it means to have a heart that chases after God's will. Is there anything on your heart today that is *chasing after His will?* How can you today walk in a manner worthy of the Lord, pleasing Him "in all respects"?

REST IN HIS LOVE

"Therefore I, the prisoner of the Lord, implore you to walk in a manner worthy of the calling with which you have been called, with all humility and gentleness, with patience, showing tolerance for one another in love, being diligent to preserve the unity of the Spirit in the bond of peace" (Ephesians 4:1-3).

delighting in the Lord

Delight yourself in the LORD;
And He will give you the desires of your heart.
PSALM 37:4

Prepare Your Heart

There was something unique about David that set him apart from the world in which he lived. It was evident that Someone unseen was the main person in his life. And that Someone was the one who made him smile. That is really what it means to delight in the Lord. It means to celebrate daily that One who brings you great joy. Just being in God's presence, walking in the light of His love, makes your heart dance and brings a smile to your face.

Do you know this kind of life? One of the great prerequisites to delighting in the Lord is that you know and walk with Him in the everyday routine of life. It is impossible to delight in someone whom you do not know by experience. To know by experience, you will need to spend hours with that person. Resolve in your heart that you will draw near and personally relate to the Lord, who is the Lover of your soul.

The heart that delights in the Lord dances in the times of darkness as well as when the sun shines. During the Civil War, a Confederate soldier was told to go kill a Union soldier who had been discovered standing guard as a sentry. As he aimed the gun at the sentry, he heard the soldier singing the words of Wesley's hymn, "Jesus, Lover of My Soul." Hearing those words, he didn't care if it was the enemy; he could not shoot. Years after the Civil War ended, there was a meeting of some of the old Confederate and Union soldiers. The Confederate soldier attended and told this story. When he was finished, an old Union soldier stood and said he was that sentry. He had been depressed and afraid when he was assigned to the isolated sentry post. So he sang the hymn to keep up his courage. Delighting in the Lord had saved his life that day.

Charles Wesley wrote "Jesus, Lover of My Soul" during a time of danger. Writing these words brought comfort to his heart as he delighted in the Lord. Meditate on the hymn as you draw near to the Lord and delight in Him today.

> Jesus, lover of my soul, let me to Thy bosom fly,
> While the nearer waters roll, while the tempest still is high.
> Hide me, O my Savior, hide, till the storm of life is past;
> Safe into the haven guide; O receive my soul at last.
>
> Other refuge have I none, hangs my helpless soul on Thee;
> Leave, ah! leave me not alone, still support and comfort me.
> All my trust on Thee is stayed, all my help from Thee I bring;
> Cover my defenseless head with the shadow of Thy wing.
>
> Wilt Thou not regard my call? Wilt Thou not accept my prayer?
> Lo! I sink, I faint, I fall—Lo! on Thee I cast my care;
> Reach me out Thy gracious hand! While I of Thy strength receive,
> Hoping against hope I stand, dying, and behold, I live.
>
> Thou, O Christ, art all I want, more than all in Thee I find;
> Raise the fallen, cheer the faint, heal the sick, and lead the blind.
> Just and holy is Thy Name, I am all unrighteousness;
> False and full of sin I am; Thou art full of truth and grace.
>
> Plenteous grace with Thee is found, grace to cover all my sin;
> Let the healing streams abound; make and keep me pure within.
> Thou of life the fountain art, freely let me take of Thee;
> Spring Thou up within my heart; rise to all eternity.

READ AND STUDY GOD'S WORD

1. David had a habit of delighting in the Lord. Read the following passages and record what you learn about David and his delight in the Lord.

1 Samuel 16:14-23

2 Samuel 6:14-16

2 Samuel 22

2. Read Psalm 37:1-9. What do you learn about David's attitude toward life? What kinds of things does he encourage you to do no matter what happens in your life? Personalize your answers. For example, "I need to trust in the Lord and do good."

3. What is the most important insight that you have learned from the Lord today in His Word?

ADORE GOD IN PRAYER

Take some time today and sing to the Lord. Choose some of your favorite worship choruses or hymns, and sing the words as a prayer to Him. You might even get a tape or CD player and go for a walk, listening to some of your favorite worship music. You may also choose to use the words of Psalm 29 to worship and delight in the Lord.

YIELD YOURSELF TO GOD

The great mark of the New Testament is that it is a dispensation of the inner life. The promise of the new covenant is: I will put my law *in their inward parts* and *in their hearts will I write it. A new heart also will I give you and a new spirit will I put within you and I will put my Spirit within you.* The promise of our Lord was *The Spirit of truth shall be in you. In that day ye shall know that I am in you.* It is in the state of one's heart that Christianity consists, in a heart into which God has sent the Spirit of His Son, a heart from which the love of God is shed abroad, that true salvation is found. The inner chamber, with its secret fellowship with the Father, who seeth in secret, is the symbol and the training school of the inner life. The true and faithful daily use of the inner chamber will make the inner hidden life strong and glad.[1]

ANDREW MURRAY IN *THE INNER LIFE*

There is nothing more important in any life than the constantly enjoyed presence of the Lord. There is nothing more vital, for without it we shall make mistakes, and without it we shall be defeated. Without the sense of His abiding presence and a place of constant communion and fellowship, how far wrong we shall go. . . . God grant that you may be found among the faithful, such as David was when he returned again to the task with sacrifice and rejoicing. May you be found among those who know the presence of the Living Christ because the blood is constantly being applied to cleanse their sinful lives. This is what brings joy and testimony to the heart![2]

ALAN REDPATH IN *THE MAKING OF A MAN OF GOD*

ENJOY HIS PRESENCE

What do you think it means to delight in the Lord? What difference do you think it makes in how you walk through your day? Record your thoughts.

REST IN HIS LOVE

"I delight greatly in the LORD; my soul rejoices in my God. For he has clothed me with garments of salvation and arrayed me in a robe of righteousness, as a bridegroom adorns his head like a priest, and as a bride adorns herself with her jewels" (Isaiah 61:10, NIV).

defending His name

"What will be done for the man who kills this Philistine and takes away the reproach
from Israel? For who is this uncircumcised Philistine, that he should taunt
the armies of the living God?"
1 SAMUEL 17:26

Prepare Your Heart

The one who has a heart that dances lives constantly in the sphere of the living God.
When this person observes that something is contrary to God, there is only one choice:
defend His name. The one who walks in the light of eternity cannot help speaking of what he or
she sees.

Samuel Rutherford was one such person. In 1627 he earned a degree from Edinburgh
College in Scotland, where he was appointed as a Professor of Humanity. In that same year,
he also became pastor of the church in Anwoth. The people in his rural congregation were
scattered in farms throughout the hill country. He had a true pastor's heart. It has been said of
him that "he was always praying, always preaching, always visiting the sick, always catechis-
ing, always writing and studying."[1]

To accomplish all that was in his heart, he got up at 3:00 every morning. He was known
as God's comforter of suffering people, probably because he was intimate with the suffering
in his own life. His wife and two of his children died during his first year at Anwoth. That
was only the beginning of his suffering.

Even though he was not a gifted speaker, his preaching had great power. One man
said that in Rutherford's preaching he saw the loveliness of Christ. Many came to hear
his messages. In 1636, Rutherford felt compelled to write a book defending the doctrine
of grace in answer to those who were saying that there is no eternal security. As a result
of his defense of the faith, he was called before the High Court of the Church of
England, stripped of his ministerial office, and exiled to Aberdeen. It broke his heart to

be separated from the congregation he loved so much.

This buffeting turned to blessing because it was from Aberdeen that he wrote the hundreds of letters that became what is known as *The Letters of Samuel Rutherford*. Charles Spurgeon, the well-known preacher, said that these letters are "the nearest thing to inspiration which can be found in all the writings of mere men." In these letters you see a heart that defends the name of the Lord in every way: in suffering, in relationships, in work, in the world. He can only speak of what he sees as his heart dances along the shores of eternity as seen in the Word of God and illumined by the Holy Spirit.

Today, as you draw near to the Lord, turn to Psalm 57 and meditate on these words that David wrote when his life was in danger. You will see the great heart that defends God's name at every turn. As you begin, ask the Lord to quiet your heart and prepare you to meet with Him today. Write below your favorite verse from Psalm 57.

READ AND STUDY GOD'S WORD

Today you will look at an event in David's life that shows what happens when God's servant comes up against those who are enemies of His Lord. David is still young, yet Samuel has already anointed him as the next king. He is so young and unassuming that he is not even allowed to fight in Israel's armies. He is basically an errand boy, sent to meet his brothers' needs, tend his father's sheep, and play the harp for Saul.

David's presence is a comfort to many because he has a heart that dances with the Lord, filled with joy and delight and with the truth of an eternal perspective. What no one knows, however, is that the heart that dances can also stand strong and steadfast in the face of great adversity. It is a heart that advances forward when everyone else retreats.

1. Read 1 Samuel 17. What stands out to you about the heart and character of David?

How does his response differ from the responses of others when confronted by Goliath?

2. Look at the following verses and record what you learn about defending the name of the Lord. Remember that God's name represents His character and ways. Be sure to personalize your answers.

Deuteronomy 32:3-4

Psalm 113:2-3

Ephesians 4:14-15

Colossians 4:5-6

1 Peter 1:13

1 Peter 3:14-17

3. In what ways has God called upon you to defend His name either through words or actions in your current circumstances?

ADORE GOD IN PRAYER

Turn to your Prayer Pages now and bring those things before the Lord that are needs in your life or in the lives of those around you. Be sure to record the date and any promises to claim related to your needs. You might take some time to review previous requests to see how God is answering your prayers. Thank the Lord for how He is working in your life and speaking to you in your time with Him. Praise His name today and thank Him for who He is and all He does.

YIELD YOURSELF TO GOD

Meditate on the words of the following letter written by Samuel Rutherford to a woman who was suffering great adversity. In this letter you will see the heart of one who knows and dances with the Lord, wants to please the Lord, and defends His name at any cost.

Think about your own response in the face of great suffering. Will you be like Paul, who said, "Suffer hardship with me, as a good soldier of Christ Jesus. No soldier in active service entangles himself in the affairs of everyday life, so that he may please the one who enlisted him as a soldier" (2 Timothy 2:3-4). If you have any thoughts about these things after you have read the following letter, record your insights in your Journal.

To the Right Honourable and Christian Lady, my Lady Kenmure Madam,—

Grace, mercy, and peace be to your Ladyship—

God be thanked you are yet in possession of Christ, and that sweet child. I pray God that the first may be a sure heritage, and the second a loan for your comfort, while you do good to His poor, afflicted, withered Mount Zion. And who knows but our Lord has comforts laid up in store for her and you! I am persuaded that Christ has bought you away from the devil, and hell, and sin, so that they have no claim to you; and that is a rich and invaluable mercy. Long since, you were half challenging death's cold kindness, in being so slow and reluctant to come to loose a tired prisoner; but you stand in need of all the crosses, losses, changes, and sad hearts that befell you since that time. Christ knows that the body of sin unsubdued will take them all, and more: we know that Paul had need of the devil's service, to buffet him; and far more we.

But, my dear and honourable Lady, spend your sand-glass well. I am sure that you have law to raise a suspension against all that devils, men, friends, worlds, losses, hell, or sin, can decree against you. It is good that your crosses will but convey you to heaven's gates: in, they cannot go; the gates shall be closed upon them, when you shall be admitted to the throne. Time does not stand still, eternity is hard at our door. Oh, what is laid up for you! Therefore, harden your face against the wind. And the Lamb, your Husband, is making ready for you. The Bridegroom is eagerly preparing for that day, as gladly as you would wish to have it yourself. He has not forgotten you.

I have heard a rumour of the prelates' purpose to banish me. But let it come, if God so wills: the other side of the sea is my Father's ground, as well as this side. I owe bowing to God, but no servile bowing to crosses: I have been but too soft in that. I am comforted that I am persuaded fully, that Christ is my partner with me in this well-born and honest cross; and if He claim right to the best half of my troubles (as I know He does to the whole), I shall remit over to Christ what I shall do in this case. I know certainly, that my Lord Jesus will not misuse nor waste my sufferings; He has use for them in His house.

Oh, what it works on me to remember that a stranger, who comes not in by the door, will build hay and stubble upon the golden foundation which I laid amongst that people at Anwoth! But I know that Providence does not squint, but looks straight through all men's darkness. Oh that I could wait upon the Lord! I had but one eye, one joy, one delight, even to preach Christ; and my mother's sons were angry at me, and have put out the poor man's one eye, and what have I behind? I am sure that this sour world has deservedly lost my heart; but oh that there were a daysman to lay his hands upon us both, and determine upon my part of it. Alas, that innocent and lovely truth should be sold! My tears are little worth, but yet for this thing I weep. I weep, alas, that my fair and lovely Lord Jesus should be misrepresented in His own house! It matters little what five hundred of me feel; yet, at the same time, faith is not drowned in me. Our King still lives. I write the prisoner's blessings: the good-will, and long-lasting kindness, with the comforts of the very God of peace, be to your Ladyship, and to your sweet child. Grace, grace be with you. Your Honour's, at all obedience, in his sweet Lord Jesus,
S. R., Aberdeen, Sept. 5, 1637[2]

ENJOY HIS PRESENCE

Close your time with the Lord today by meditating on the words of this hymn written by Luther B. Bridges, entitled "There's Within My Heart a Melody."

There's within my heart a melody
Jesus whispers sweet and low:
Fear not, I am with thee, peace, be still,
in all of life's ebb and flow.

Refrain:
Jesus, Jesus, Jesus,
sweetest name I know,
fills my every longing,
keeps me singing as I go.

All my life was wrecked by sin and strife,
discord filled my heart with pain;
Jesus swept across the broken strings,
stirred the slumbering chords again.

Refrain

Though sometimes he leads through waters deep,
trials fall across the way,

though sometimes the path seems rough and steep,
see his footprints all the way.

Refrain

Feasting on the riches of his grace,
resting 'neath his sheltering wing,
always looking on his smiling face,
that is why I shout and sing.

Refrain

Soon he's coming back to welcome me
far beyond the starry sky;
I shall wing my flight to worlds unknown;
I shall reign with him on high.

Refrain

Will you praise His name today and worship Him in everything you do?

REST IN HIS LOVE

"Let the name of the LORD be praised, both now and forevermore. From the rising of the sun to the place where it sets, the name of the LORD is to be praised" (Psalm 113:2-3, NIV).

inquiring of the Lord

Then it came about afterwards that David inquired of the LORD.
2 SAMUEL 2:1

Prepare Your Heart

D avid stands out as a bright, shining star in the Bible. He is one of the Lord's great heroes. In *The Making of a Man of God*, Alan Redpath points out that the Bible never flatters its heroes. That is so true. The biblical writers are candid about David's glaring faults and sins. Yet despite those sins, David's heart is so crystal clear in its love and reverence for the living God. His attitude is especially apparent when his actions are contrasted with those of his predecessor, Saul.

Saul constantly did whatever he wanted to do, without asking God. When he and his armies defeated the Amalekites (1 Samuel 15), instead of destroying everything as he had been instructed to do by the prophet Samuel, he spared the king and the best of the animals and material possessions. Now, that might seem like no big thing in the eyes of men. But listen to what God had to say about it: "I regret that I have made Saul king, for he has turned back from following Me and has not carried out My commands" (1 Samuel 15:11). Can you see how imperative it is to know what God thinks in any situation? How sad it would be to hear God say that He *regrets* anything to do with us.

The worst part about this was Saul's attitude following the deed. After he disobeyed the Lord, he told Samuel, "Blessed are you of the LORD! I have carried out the command of the LORD" (1 Samuel 15:13). When Samuel confronted him, Saul defended himself by saying, "I did obey the voice of the LORD, and went on the mission on which the LORD sent me, and have brought back Agag the king of Amalek, and have utterly destroyed the Amalekites. But the people took some of the spoil, sheep and oxen, the choicest of the things devoted to destruction, to sacrifice to the LORD your God at Gilgal" (1 Samuel 15:20-21). Saul called Him "the LORD your God." How true that was. If He were Saul's Lord, Saul would have endeavored to discover how he could please Him.

You may be thinking that perhaps Saul did not know what he was doing. But he did. When Samuel confronted him, he said, "I have sinned; I have indeed transgressed the command of the LORD and your words, because I feared the people and listened to their voice" (1 Samuel 15:24).

That was only one of Saul's many actions that betrayed a heart that was more concerned with pleasing self and the people than God. Saul was headstrong and often rushed to action without waiting for God. Once he even offered a burnt offering to God instead of waiting for Samuel. Samuel told Saul, "Now your kingdom shall not endure. The LORD has sought out for Himself a man after His own heart, and the LORD has appointed him as a ruler over His people, because you have not kept what the LORD commanded you" (1 Samuel 13:14).

Today your goal is to discover a heart very different from that of Saul. In the heart that dances with the Lord, there is a reverence that always asks. This heart is humble, free from presumption, and willing to wait for the Lord to act on its behalf. Will you ask God today to give you such a heart?

How exciting it is when God makes the moves and is the author of the work in your life! His ideas are the very best, and He is waiting to carry out His purposes in your life today.

As you begin your time with the Lord, turn to Psalm 4, written by David. What is your favorite phrase in this psalm?

READ AND STUDY GOD'S WORD

1. David was very different from Saul. Look at the following events in David's life and record what you learn about his approach to each circumstance.

1 Samuel 23:1-5

1 Samuel 30:6-8

2 Samuel 2:1

2 Samuel 5:17-25

1 Chronicles 17

Summarize in one or two sentences what you have learned from the life of David.

2. The heart that honors the Lord is willing to ask God and wait for Him. This kind of approach to life is found throughout Scripture, especially in the words of the psalmists. Look at the following verses and record your insights.
   Psalm 38:15

Psalm 130:5-6

Jeremiah 33:3

ADORE GOD IN PRAYER

In what areas of your life are you tempted to rush out and make something happen just to solve a problem? Where is there a need for you to draw near and ask the Lord what to do? Are you willing then to wait for Him to make the path clear? Write a prayer in your Journal today, expressing all that is on your heart.

YIELD YOURSELF TO GOD

The help of God does not come to us when we are indifferent. It comes to the man who is depending on God in the thick of the fight. It comes to the one who tarries for the vision in faith. It comes to the one who believes that he who waits upon the Lord shall never be confounded. It comes to the one who rests upon the promises of the Word. It comes to the one who believes that before he calls, God will answer. It comes to the man who lives by faith as if in the actual possession of the answer to his prayer, although the enemy is still around him. It is faith which turns distress into singing.[1]

ALAN REDPATH IN *THE MAKING OF A MAN OF GOD*

Are you so identified with the Lord's life that you are simply a child of God, continu-ally talking to Him and realizing that all things come from His hands? Is the Eternal child in you living in the Father's house? Are the graces of His ministering life working out through you in your home, in your business, in your domestic circle? Have you been wondering why you are going through the things you are? It is not that you have to go through them, it is because of the relation into which the Son of God has come in His Father's providence in your particular sainthood. Let Him have His way, keep in perfect union with Him. The vicarious life of your Lord is to become your vital simple life; the way He worked and lived among men must be the way He lives in you.[2]

OSWALD CHAMBERS IN *MY UTMOST FOR HIS HIGHEST*

If you begin with God, your enemies grow small. If you begin with the enemy, you may never reach God. If you begin with Him, the problems begin to dwindle: if you begin with the problems, you never get through to God. . . . Are you in doubt? One voice may say to you, *Come this way.* Prudence may suggest to you one thing, faith another. Worldly wisdom says *this* path, but the voice of the Spirit says *that* path. If you are not sure, get alone somewhere with God until every other voice is silent and all human opinions are shut out, and learn to look to the Lord.[3]

ALAN REDPATH IN *THE MAKING OF A MAN OF GOD*

ENJOY HIS PRESENCE

Is your heart one that turns to the Lord to ask Him what to do? If so, then those times are sweet indeed, as you fellowship with the One who loves you most. Close your time with the Lord by thinking about these words written by William Walford:

Sweet hour of prayer! sweet hour of prayer!
that calls me from a world of care,
and bids me at my Father's throne
make all my wants and wishes known.
In seasons of distress and grief,
my soul has often found relief,
and oft escaped the tempter's snare
by thy return, sweet hour of prayer!

Sweet hour of prayer! sweet hour of prayer!
the joys I feel, the bliss I share
of those whose anxious spirits burn
with strong desires for thy return!
With such I hasten to the place

where God my Savior shows his face,
and gladly take my station there,
and wait for thee, sweet hour of prayer!

Sweet hour of prayer! sweet hour of prayer!
thy wings shall my petition bear
to him whose truth and faithfulness
engage the waiting soul to bless.
And since he bids me seek his face,
believe his word, and trust his grace,
I'll cast on him my every care,
and wait for thee, sweet hour of prayer!

REST IN HIS LOVE

"Don't worry over anything whatever; tell God every detail of your needs in earnest and thankful prayer, and the peace of God which transcends human understanding, will keep constant guard over your hearts and minds as they rest in Christ Jesus" (Philippians 4:6-7, PH).

for sheer joy

"I will celebrate before the LORD."
2 SAMUEL 6:21

Prepare Your Heart

Have you ever watched people dance who seem to know each other's moves? One leads, the other follows, but the movements are effortless. In the 1984 Olympics in Sarajevo, Torvill and Dean stunned the world with their flawless dance on ice to Ravel's "Bolero." The performance so impressed the judges that the couple received twelve perfect scores and won the gold medal. What stood out the most in their ice dance was the precision and synchronization. Never once were they out of step with each other. No matter what the music played, they moved smoothly and effortlessly.

The Lord desires to lead you in the dance of life. As you move with Him, your heart will dance in joy and celebration of His very real presence with you. His presence in your life does not mean an absence of difficulty or pain. But, with His life in you, He will overcome whatever you face.

Today as you think about the heart that dances in your study of intimacy with the Lord, write a prayer to Him, asking Him to show you how to dance and keep in step with Him.

READ AND STUDY GOD'S WORD

We have been looking at the life of David. Now that you have spent so many days immersed in his life, you probably feel as though you know him. Someday you will have the opportunity to talk with David in heaven! And you will see so many other saints of God who were intimate with the Lord.

1. One event stands out as a definitive picture of David expressing a heart that knew how to dance in the presence of his living Lord. Turn to 2 Samuel 6 and record all that you see about how David worshiped the Lord.

2. To celebrate the Lord means in the Hebrew to sing, dance, and make music to the Lord. In the New Testament, Paul tells us to "speak to one another with psalms, hymns and spiritual songs. Sing and make music in your heart to the Lord, always giving thanks to God the Father for everything, in the name of our Lord Jesus Christ" (Ephesians 5:19-20, NIV). In these exhortations you see a lifestyle of joy. Look at the following verses and record what you learn about joy and rejoicing. Personalize your answers.

Nehemiah 8:10

John 15:11; 16:22

Romans 12:15

Philippians 4:4

3. Where do we find the ability and strength to rejoice even in the midst of suffering? Look at the following verses and record your insights. Be sure to personalize your observations and insights.

Acts 17:28

Galatians 5:22-25

Philippians 4:13

4. What is your favorite insight from your time with God in His Word today?

ADORE GOD IN PRAYER

What gives you cause to rejoice today? Name those things to the Lord and thank Him for His presence in your life. He is your living God and desires to lead you in life today. God bless you as you continue on in the great adventure of knowing Him.

YIELD YOURSELF TO GOD

The joy of the Lord is something that rises above circumstances and focuses on the very character of God. I learned that there is a holy joy, so pure it exists even in the midst of sorry circumstances. I also learned that joy comes to us from the Holy Spirit along with love, peace, and other virtues described by Paul in his letter to the Galatians. But how do the commentators say this joy expresses itself in the Bible? Here I was really surprised. In *dancing, shouting, singing, clapping, leaping, foot-stamping, feasting and celebrating*. For example, in the week-long harvest Feast of Booths or Tabernacles, the Hebrews took to the open air, living in the shade of booths made of the leafy fronds of trees. They did so in sheer gladness of heart as a way of thanksgiving, in obedience to Deuteronomy 16:15: "You shall be altogether joyful."[1]

SHERWOOD E. WIRT IN *JESUS MAN OF JOY*

A story told by Brennan Manning describes a lonely high school girl named Jenny:

She was not a pretty girl; Jenny described herself as "ugly." Because high school teens tend to be as shallow as we adults, Jenny's life was miserable. She went to all the school dances, but none of the boys ever asked to dance with her. The other girls teased her mercilessly and the boys often "set her up" by raising her hopes for a date and then cruelly tricking her.

One night Jenny cried herself to sleep after attending a school dance. She dressed up in her prettiest clothes, put on her makeup, and went with high hopes that some-one would finally ask her to dance. All through the dance she sat on a chair, next to the wall, alone. A couple of times her heart leapt when a boy would approach her direction, only to be broken when he would ask one of the other girls to dance. Bitter tears drenched her pillow that night. Anger, bitterness and pain rocked her to sleep.

Jenny then tells the remarkable story of a fascinating dream that came over her that night. In her dream she was at a dance. The magnificent dance hall was decorated just so. Silver balls hung from the ceiling, scattering flashing bits of light over the crowd. The men were dressed in tuxedos. The women were dressed in beautiful formal gowns adorned with orchid corsages. And there was Jenny, dressed in her finest, standing along the wall, alone.

Suddenly the doors swung open and in strode the most handsome man she had ever seen. He was so beautiful that all the dancers stopped in mid-step and stared at him. He made his way across the dance floor to where Jenny was standing. With a smile on his face he looked into her eyes, held out his hand and said, "Jenny, will you dance with me?"

At first she was stunned, then disbelieving. She looked around the crowd to see if it was a setup. She'd been cruelly tricked like this before. But this beautiful man looked directly into her eyes and said, "Jenny, I'd like to dance with you."

Jenny didn't know how to dance. No one had ever asked her before. She felt clumsy and awkward as the handsome stranger whisked her to the dance floor! He took her in his arms and began to lead. She was thrilled to discover that following his lead freed her to dance with abandon. She was free as a bird, smooth as a cat. She could dance! Her soul overflowed with joy.

"I've wanted to dance with you for a long time, Jenny," the stranger said. She could hardly believe what she was hearing! Then she heard him say, "I love you, Jenny. I love you with all my heart and all my soul and all my strength." She turned and looked him in the eyes. She could see his passion, his unconditional love, and suddenly she knew the name of this beautiful stranger who had asked her to dance. She was dancing with Jesus.

Jesus doesn't care if you're ugly. He doesn't care if you're fat or thin. He doesn't care about the horrible sins and crimes you've committed—that's why He died on the Cross. He simply loves you and wants to dance with you. If you will let him lead he will fill your life with joy.[2]

Enjoy His Presence

Will you dance with the Lord today as you go about your day? In what ways can you "keep in step" with the Spirit of God in the things He has called you to do today? Close by writing a prayer in your Journal, expressing all that is on your heart.

Rest in His Love

"Since we live by the Spirit, let us keep in step with the Spirit" (Galatians 5:25, NIV).

DEAR FRIEND,

The next two days are your opportunity to spend time reviewing what you have learned this week. You may wish to write your thoughts and insights in your Journal. As you think about what you have learned about a heart that dances, write:

Your most significant insight:

Your favorite quote:

Your favorite verse:

Close this week by meditating on these words by A. W. Tozer:

When the apostle cries *that I may know Him*, he uses the word *know* not in its intellectual but in its experiential sense. We must look for the meaning—not to the mind but to the heart. Theological knowledge is knowledge about God. While this is indispensable it is not sufficient. It bears the same relation to man's spiritual need as a well does to the need of his physical body. It is not the rock-lined pit for which the dusty traveler longs, but the sweet, cool water that flows up from it. It is not intellectual knowledge about God that quenches man's ancient heart-thirst, but the Person and Presence of God Himself. These come to us through Christian doctrine, but they are more than doctrine. Christian truth is designed to lead us to God, not to serve as a substitute for God.[1]

A. W. TOZER IN "KEYS TO THE DEEPER LIFE"

finding your treasure in life

week
five

MARY

when life surprises you

And Mary said, "Behold, the bondslave of the Lord;
may it be done to me according to your word."
LUKE 1:38

Prepare Your Heart

In every circumstance of life you are faced with two choices. You can either respond or react. Response is determined from within; reaction is determined from without—by the circumstances. Response relies on the truth of God's Word and results in the fulfillment of God's plan for your life. Reaction is often hasty and can have disastrous consequences. Intimacy with God will depend on your responses in life.

Mary had a uniquely intimate relationship with the Lord. She was privileged to give birth to Jesus, the Son of God who would save His people from their sins. Not only is He the Son, He is also King of kings and Lord of lords, Creator of the universe, and the promised Messiah.

Nothing in Mary's life went the way she had dreamed. That may be true for you also. The question for you today is, Do you *respond* or *react* in the circumstances of life? Your decisions will determine the depth of your intimacy with God. Your decision to respond will be determined by how you regard the Person, words, ways, and works of God Himself. Is He your great treasure in life? Discovering that He is your treasure in every circumstance is the goal this week.

As you begin your time with the Lord today, turn to Psalm 59. What do you see about David's heart and attitude in this psalm?

READ AND STUDY GOD'S WORD

Today you begin looking at the life of Mary, the mother of Jesus. The first circumstance of Mary's life to think about occurred in a village called Nazareth in Galilee. If you travel along a plain formed by the mountains of lower Galilee, you will be in a valley that widens until, after an hour's journey, you arrive at an enclosure that seems to be a sanctuary of nature. Fifteen hill-tops surround this stretch of land. On the lower slopes of the tallest mountain—some five hundred feet high—resides the small town of Nazareth. The surrounding hills are fragrant with aromatic plants and bright with richly colored flowers. It is a scene of tranquil beauty.

In Mary's day, Nazareth was one of the small towns where the priests would gather in preparation for their service in the temple. It was also a crossroads for secular traffic. The caravan route led right through the town, bringing men of all nations to its streets. The people of Nazareth were outspoken, hot-blooded, and brave.

Mary was a simple teenager about to marry a man named Joseph. It was probably one of the most exciting times of her life. Because they were betrothed to one another, their relationship was more binding than an engagement. A betrothal could be terminated only by a divorce. Things did not go as Mary had planned. Something happened that transformed her life.

1. In his gospel, Luke recorded things that are not in any of the other gospels. He shared things that only Mary could have known. He shared what went on in her heart. It is thought that Mary told Luke these things to include in his gospel. Read Luke 1:26-38. Record your insights about what happened to Mary and how she responded.

2. Read Luke 1:39-56. What do you see in these verses about Mary's heart for the Lord?

3. Mary said in Luke 1:38, "Behold, the bondslave of the Lord; may it be done to me according to your word." What was she really saying?

4. Do you have the kind of heart that prompts such a statement as Mary's when you are surprised by the circumstances of life? Record your thoughts.

5. How do you think a response like Mary's makes a difference in one's intimacy with the Lord?

6. What can you count on in every situation to enable you to surrender to the Lord as Mary did? Read the following verses and record your insights.
    Psalm 84:11-12

    Isaiah 55:8-9

    Lamentations 3:21-26

    Romans 8:28

ADORE GOD IN PRAYER

Talk with the Lord today as you would with a friend who loves and accepts you as you are. Are there surprises in your life right now that you don't understand or that threaten to discourage you? Think about Mary and what it must have been like for her to have her life turned upside down that day when the angel Gabriel made his announcement. Take these circumstances and people to the Lord and ask Him to work out His purposes in your life. Ask Him to give you a heart that says, "Behold, the bondslave of the Lord; may it be done to me according to your word."

YIELD YOURSELF TO GOD

If we wholly trust an interest to God, we must keep our hands off it; and He will guard it for us better than we can help Him. *Rest in the Lord, and wait patiently for him: fret not thyself because of him who prospereth in his way, because of the man who bringeth wicked devices to pass.* Things may seem to be going all wrong, but He knows as well as we; and He will arise in the right moment if we are really trusting Him so fully, as to let Him work in His own way and time. There is nothing so masterly as inactivity in some things, and there is nothing so hurtful as restless working, for God has undertaken to work His sovereign will (A. B. Simpson).[1]

MRS. CHARLES COWMAN IN *STREAMS IN THE DESERT*

Is there one who is facing something that seems impossible? Does the appointed burden feel too heavy to be carried? The disappointment too sharp to be welcomed? The duty too toilsome to be performed with joy? *You have not to do it in your unaided strength: it is God who is all the while supplying the impulse, giving you the power to resolve, the strength to perform, the execution of His good pleasure* (Phil. 2:13, Way). And so, *I am equal to every lot, through the help of Him who gives me inward strength* (Phil. 4:13, Way). . . . All the tremendous forces of nature in the world today are at the call of our God, and are only a faint shadow of the spiritual power that is His, and that He is ready to put forth for us. Is it not amazing? How utterly foolish it is to plead weakness when we, even we, may (if we will), move into the stream of that very power.[2]

AMY CARMICHAEL IN *THOU GIVEST, THEY GATHER*

ENJOY HIS PRESENCE

Close your time with the Lord today by thinking about your most significant insights. What stood out to you in the example of Mary, the passages of Scripture, and the devotional readings? Write a prayer to the Lord in your Journal, expressing all that is on your heart related to what He has shown you today.

REST IN HIS LOVE

"'The LORD is my portion,' says my soul, 'therefore I have hope in Him'" (Lamentations 3:24).

when you hear God's promise

But Mary treasured up all these things, pondering them in her heart.
LUKE 2:19

Prepare Your Heart

Mary had a habit that made the difference throughout her life. When she heard God speak or saw Him work in a powerful way, she "treasured . . . these things, pondering them in her heart." That is why she is such a good example of a heart that dances. The question for you today is, How do you respond to what God says in His Word? Have you learned the art of treasuring God's Word and pondering what He says? Because Mary did this, the Lord became her great treasure in life. As a result, she enjoyed a deep intimacy with Him. And He chose her for a very important task.

Perhaps God has chosen you for a task as part of His purposes for you and for others around you. Have you learned this great secret of response to God's Word? Will you slow down today to listen to God speak in His Word?

Begin your quiet time by meditating on Psalm 1. What are the two different ways a person can live, and what are the results of each way of life?

READ AND STUDY GOD'S WORD

When the time came for Mary's baby to be born, Joseph and Mary were in Bethlehem, far from Nazareth. They could find no place to stay in Bethlehem except a stable. That was where Jesus was born.

1. Everyone was interested in this child. Turn to Luke 2:1-40. How did different people respond to the birth of Jesus?

2. What do you think it might have been like for Mary when Jesus was born?

3. In Jesus' birth, how do you see that Mary's heart loved the Lord?

4. Describe in your own words what it means to treasure what God says.

5. What does God say about taking time with what He says in His Word?
   Joshua 1:8

   Psalm 1:2

   Psalm 119:97-99

6. What is your favorite way to take time with the Word of God and to think about what it means?

ADORE GOD IN PRAYER

Have you ever taken the Word of God and used it in your conversation with the Lord? Turn to the Psalms and personalize the words, praying them to the Lord. You may choose your favorite psalm or just begin with Psalm 25. Take as much time as you have, talking with God.

YIELD YOURSELF TO GOD

> If it is God's Word, revealing His will, nothing could be of greater importance than understanding it. If the Bible was given to reveal the truth and not to hide it, God must intend that we understand it.[1]
>
> J. ROBERTSON MCQUILKIN IN *UNDERSTANDING AND APPLYING THE BIBLE*

> The Bible is one book, one history, one story, His story. Behind 10,000 events stands God, the builder of history, the maker of the ages. Eternity bounds the one side, eternity bounds the other side, and time is in between: Genesis—origins, Revelation—endings, and all the way between, God is working things out. You can go down into the minutest detail everywhere and see that there is one great purpose moving through the ages: the eternal design of the Almighty God to redeem a wrecked and ruined world. . . . We must come to it in a common sense fashion. Believe that every book is about something and read and reread until you find out what that something is. . . . Read it seeking for illumination. It is a revelation and He will flash light upon the page as you come humbly.[2]
>
> HENRIETTA MEARS IN *WHAT THE BIBLE IS ALL ABOUT*

> Meditation is the activity of calling to mind, and thinking over, and dwelling on, and applying to oneself, the various things that one knows about the works and ways and purposes and promises of God. It is an activity of holy thought, consciously performed in the presence of God, under the eye of God, by the help of God, as a means of communion with God.[3]
>
> J. I. PACKER IN *KNOWING GOD*

Devotional study is not so much a technique as a spirit. It is the spirit of eagerness which seeks the mind of God; it is the spirit of humility which listens readily to the voice of God; it is the spirit of adventure which pursues earnestly the will of God; it is the spirit of adoration which rests in the presence of God. . . . The object of devotional study is to find a center around which thought and conduct may be integrated in terms of holiness and service. Since the Scriptures are the message of God, their teaching by precept and by example will provide that center, and its applicability will be determined by its analogy with the existing situation.[4]

MERRILL C. TENNEY IN GALATIANS

ENJOY HIS PRESENCE

How important is God's Word in your life? Do you have an eagerness and a reverence as you approach it each day? Are you willing to slow down and take time to think about what God is saying to you in His Word? What is the most important truth to you in your quiet time with the Lord today? Summarize in one or two sentences what the Lord has shown you.

REST IN HIS LOVE

"This book of the law shall not depart from your mouth, but you shall meditate on it day and night, so that you may be careful to do according to all that is written in it; for then you will make your way prosperous, and then you will have success" (Joshua 1:8).

when you don't understand

And He went down with them and came to Nazareth, and He continued in subjection
to them; and His mother treasured all these things in her heart.

LUKE 2:51

Prepare Your Heart

In your journey of intimacy with the Lord, there are times when He will seem foreign to
you. Things will happen in your life that have no explanation. And you will wonder, *What
is the Lord doing?* The thought will come to you that you truly know very little about Him.
What you have learned to this point will seem as nothing compared to what God wants to
show you about Himself. This is the way of intimacy with the Lord. At times it is a solitary
journey. Why? Because the Lord is building something deep and intimate and personal
between you and Himself. He wants to be your great treasure in life.

Catherine Marshall was married to the well-known Scottish preacher Peter Marshall.
One day she was speaking to a group of women at a church and became dizzy. She spent
three days undergoing tests at a Baltimore hospital. The diagnosis: tuberculosis. She was
stunned. The treatment was to stay at home in bed until she became well.

The doctors could not predict how long it would take for her illness to resolve. Eighteen
months came and went, and Catherine was still in bed with no improvement. She went to
five of the top specialists in the field, and their recommendations were the same: wait and
rest. This was a time of great soul-searching for Catherine. She opened her Bible and began
to seek out exactly who the Lord is and what He could do in her life. It was as though she
was learning about Him for the first time. She studied God's love. She poured out her heart
in confession of sin to Him. She then began asking God to make her well. She felt as though
her faith was becoming stronger. When the next set of diagnostic X-rays were completed,
there was no change.

One day her husband handed her a pamphlet. In it was the story of a missionary who had been bedridden for eight years. The missionary described how she prayed and begged God for healing. She then told how she was brought to a different kind of prayer. In surrender she prayed, "Lord, I give in. If I am to be sick for the rest of my life, I bow to Thy will. I want Thee even more than I want health. It is for Thee to decide."[1] The missionary experienced a peace she had not known for eight years. Within two weeks she was able to get out of bed, completely well.

Catherine learned something powerful in this reading, which seemed to mirror her own life. She learned what she called "the prayer of relinquishment." She said to the Lord, "I've done everything I've known how to do, and it hasn't been good enough. I'm desperately weary of the struggle of trying to persuade You to give me what I want. I'm beaten, whipped, through. If you want me to be an invalid for the rest of my life, all right. Here I am. Do anything You like with me and my life."[2] Following this prayer, Catherine experienced a deep peace. Early the next morning, she sensed the presence of the Lord with her in a way that she had not known before. She believed her recovery began at that moment, until finally she was healed of tuberculosis. It was a long process, for the Lord had many things to show her about Himself. However, it was that prayer of relinquishment that began the process.

You have been looking at the life of Mary, the mother of Jesus. You have seen that Mary's life did not go in the way she may have hoped or dreamed. Yet the Lord was her great treasure. When things happened to her that seemed strange, she "treasured these things in her heart." Today you are going to look at another traumatic event in her life. It was a time when she didn't understand the ways of the Lord. She had to relinquish her own understanding to God and rely on His strength to carry her through.

As you begin this time with the Lord, turn to Psalm 91 and write down your insights.

READ AND STUDY GOD'S WORD

1. Read Luke 2:40-52. Describe what happened to Mary.

2. What do you think Mary felt when she couldn't find her son in the caravan?

3. What was Mary's response after this experience?

4. In what ways do you think Mary had to trust God and surrender to Him?

5. To surrender all to God is a sign of trust. What does it mean to trust God? Look at the following verses and record your insights about trusting God. Be sure to personalize your answers. For example, "I am not to trust in earthly things."
   Job 13:15

   Psalm 9:10

   Psalm 44:5-8

   Proverbs 3:5-6

   Luke 1:45

6. Can you relate to the experiences of Mary or of Catherine Marshall? Has there ever been a time when you have not understood God? If so, what have you learned to do in such times?

ADORE GOD IN PRAYER

Will you pray a prayer similar to the one Catherine Marshall prayed, laying everything at the Lord's feet? Turn to your Journal and write a prayer to the Lord. Pour out your heart to Him, giving Him those things that seem to grip your soul and cause you pain and worry. Leave them in the hands of the Lord today.

YIELD YOURSELF TO GOD

Faith by its very nature must be tried, and the real trial of faith is not that we find it difficult to trust God, but that God's character has to be cleared in our own minds. Faith in its actual working out has to go through spells of unsyllabled isolation. Never confound the trial of faith with the ordinary discipline of life, much that we call the trial of faith is the inevitable result of being alive. Faith in the Bible is faith in God against everything that contradicts Him—I will remain true to God's character whatever He may do. *Though He slay me, yet will I trust Him*—this is the most sublime utterance of faith in the whole of the Bible.[3]

OSWALD CHAMBERS IN *MY UTMOST FOR HIS HIGHEST*

When God wants to drill a man,
and thrill a man,
and skill a man
to play the noblest part;
when He yearns with all His heart
to create so great and bold a man
that all the world shall be amazed,
watch His methods, watch His ways!
How He ruthlessly perfects
Whom He royally elects!
How He hammers him and hurts him,
And with mighty blows converts him

Into trial shapes of clay which
Only God understands;
While his tortured heart is crying
And he lifts beseeching hands!
How he bends but never breaks
When his good He undertakes;
How He uses whom He chooses,
And with every purpose fuses him;
By every act induces him
To try his splendor out—
God knows what He's about.

AUTHOR UNKNOWN

ENJOY HIS PRESENCE

What is your most significant insight today? How can you carry what you have learned with you throughout the day? How will it make a difference in your life today?

REST IN HIS LOVE

"For we do not have a high priest who cannot sympathize with our weaknesses, but One who has been tempted in all things as we are, yet without sin. Therefore let us draw near with confidence to the throne of grace, so that we may receive mercy and find grace to help in time of need" (Hebrews 4:15-16).

when you are in need

When the wine ran out, the mother of Jesus said to Him, "They have no wine."
JOHN 2:3

Prepare Your Heart

Corrie ten Boom and her sister, Betsie, sat with their father listening to the Dutch prime minister promise that they did not need to worry about being attacked by the Germans. Their father turned off the radio and told his daughters that the prime minister was wrong and that indeed Germany would attack Holland. He was right. Before long, their peaceful town of Haarlem was filled with German soldiers. Curfews were set and ration cards for food were dispensed. The freedoms they knew were slowly taken away.

What would you do if such a thing happened in your city or town? It seems impossible. Yet perhaps you have experienced something similar. Perhaps your life is nothing like what you had hoped. You find yourself in a place of great need. What are you to do?

Corrie ten Boom did what her father had taught her to do. She prayed. In every situation, no matter how small or large, she cried out to the Lord. As a result, she found the Lord to be an ever-present help in times of need.

At one point, Corrie needed to know where she could get ration cards. She asked the Lord, and He showed her the way. When the Gestapo stormed their house and took Corrie into a room and began questioning her and hitting her, she cried out, "Lord Jesus, help me!" A policeman told her that if she used that name again, he would kill her. He then stopped beating her and took her back to where her family was.

When she was arrested and taken for a hearing to determine her sentence, she prayed, "Lord Jesus, you were questioned too. Please show me what to do." During the questioning, an officer asked her about her activities, and she told him about her work with the mentally handicapped. He told her that such work was a waste of time. She began to tell him about God's love. She told him that God looks at things differently than man does. When she said

157

these words, he ended the questioning for the day. The next day the hearing resumed, and the officer asked Corrie more about God and the Bible. Corrie was able to tell him about the hope and forgiveness found in Jesus Christ. While this officer did not have the power to set her family free, he did help the ten Booms as much as possible.

In spite of his help, Corrie and Betsie ten Boom were taken to Ravensbruck concentration camp. The conditions were horrifying. Fourteen hundred women were housed in a room meant to hold four hundred. There were constant fights among the women. Betsie prayed that God would give peace to the barracks where they were housed. Soon they began to see a change in the atmosphere. At night Corrie and Betsie read and taught from the Bible. Many women attended their meetings. The guards avoided their barracks because of the fleas in the straw mattresses. Corrie and Betsie thanked the Lord for the fleas.

Every day the women lived in fear as to whether that day would be the day their name was called and they would be led to their death. One day during roll call, Corrie heard her name called. She wondered what would happen and prayed, "Father in heaven, please help me now." Betsie had died of illness the week before. Now perhaps it was Corrie's turn. She reported to the officer at Ravensbruck and was handed a card stamped with the word *Entlassen*—Released. She was given her possessions, some new clothes, and a railway pass back to Holland. Later she learned that her release had been a mistake. One week after she left, all the women of her age in the camp were killed.

Corrie used to say that "faith is like a radar that sees through the fog—the reality of things at a distance that the human eye cannot see."[1] She said, "Never be afraid to trust an unknown future to a known God."[2] She lived what she taught. She showed her trust by crying out to God through every circumstance.

Have you learned this secret when you are in need? Today, as you begin your time with the Lord, write a prayer below or in your Journal. Ask the Lord to quiet your heart and speak to you in the areas where you have a need. You may always pour out all that is on your heart and soul to the Lord.

READ AND STUDY GOD'S WORD

1. The Lord was Mary's treasure. Because of that, she knew exactly where to run in times of need. Turn to John 2:1-11. Describe what the need was, what Mary did, and what happened as a result.

2. The Scriptures consistently portray God as a help in a time of need. How can God help? Record your insights about the Lord's help as you look at the following verses.
   Genesis 16:1-15

   Judges 16:17-31 (the example of Samson)

   2 Chronicles 14:8-15 (the example of Asa)

   Psalm 121

   Matthew 15:22-28 (the example of the Canaanite woman)

   Luke 18:27

   Hebrews 4:16

3. Summarize in one or two sentences what is most significant to you today from your time in God's Word.

ADORE GOD IN PRAYER

Guide me, O Thou great Jehovah,
pilgrim through this barren land;
I am weak, but Thou art mighty
Hold me with Thy powerful hand:
Bread of heaven, Bread of heaven,
Feed me 'til I want no more,
Feed me 'til I want no more.

Open now the crystal fountain,
Whence the healing stream doth flow;
Let the fire and cloudy pillar
Lead me all my journey through:
Strong Deliverer, strong Deliverer,
Be Thou still my strength and shield,
Be Thou still my strength and shield.

When I reach the river Jordan,
Bid my anxious fears subside;
Bear me through the swelling current,
Land me safe on Canaan's side:
Songs of praises, songs of praises
I will ever give to Thee,
I will ever give to Thee.

WILLIAM WILLIAMS

YIELD YOURSELF TO GOD

The mother of Jesus reveals herself as a tried and true woman of prayer. In the first place, she goes to the right place with the need she has become acquainted with. She goes to Jesus and tells Him everything. In the next place, notice what she says to Jesus. Just these few simple words, *They have no wine.* Note here what prayer is. To pray is to tell

Jesus what we lack. Intercession is to tell Jesus what we see that others lack. . . . When the answer is not forthcoming at once, we think that we must do something in addition to that which we have already done before God can hear us. Just what this something is, we are not certain of in our own minds. . . . All this is changed when we, like the mother of Jesus, learn to know Him so well that we feel safe when we have left our difficulties with Him. To know Jesus in this way is a prerequisite of all true prayer. This, therefore, is what the Spirit of prayer tries to teach us. It is His work to explain Christ to us and glorify Him (John 16:14). As we learn to know Jesus in this way better and better, our prayers become quiet, confidential and blessed conversations with Him, our Best Friend, about the things that are on our minds, whether it be our own needs or the needs of others. We experience wonderful peace and security by leaving our difficulties, both great and small, with Him, who is not only solicitous for our welfare but who also understands what is best for us. And especially will our prayer life become restful when it really dawns upon us that we have done all we are supposed to do when we have spoken to Him about it. From that moment we have left it with Him. It is His responsibility then, if we dare use such a childlike expression. And that we dare to do![3]

O. HALLESBY IN *PRAYER*

I never grow weary of emphasizing our helplessness, for it is the decisive factor not only in our prayer life, but in our whole relationship to God. As long as we are conscious of our helplessness we will not be overtaken by any difficulty, disturbed by any distress or frightened by any hindrance. We will expect nothing of ourselves and therefore bring all our difficulties and hindrances to God in prayer. And this means to open the door unto Him and to give God the opportunity to help us in our helplessness by means of the miraculous powers which are at His disposal.[4]

O. HALLESBY IN *PRAYER*

God indeed gives many things simply because He is God, and a God of grace. He sends His rain on the just and the unjust. He has general blessings which He pours out whether we pray or not. But there are great and special bounties which He holds in reserve for those who pray, which he bestows because of our importunity. It is like this. Here are the heavens overarching us. They are always full of the moisture which is ready to descend in the form of rain. That rain is always, as it were, hanging over the heads of the children of men. But it does not descend in the form of rain until a cool current of air meets the moisture-laden clouds and condenses them into showers at that particular point. So these special gifts of God are, as it were, His clouds hung over us big with promise waiting for our stream of prayer to rise and condense them into showers of blessing, but if we pray not they float by leaving us unvisited, unrefreshed. We have a beautiful illustration of this truth in Samson's life (Judges 15:18-19). Samson had just won a great victory in the slaughter of a thousand of his enemies. He finds himself weary, and sore athirst. God looks down upon him and sees his condition but there is no deliverance recorded until Samson *called on the Lord*. Then God's hand clave the earth and the living water gushed forth to revive and save the earnest petitioner. . . . How true this is in our lives! We come into some place of stress in life. The gloom is thick; the burden is heavy; the voice of hope is faint; the vision of faith is dimmed. While we are thirsty, God is waiting—waiting for our cry to Him. The very ground beneath our feet is throbbing with the pulse of the thirst-slaking fountain that is ready to spurt forth when we cry. But if we do not cry we have not well, for it is *the well of him that cries*. Sometimes men shoot an oil well with a cartridge that spurts the fluid into the air by its force. So prayer is God's well opener. When we cry, the earth cleaves and the fountain bursts forth. Prayer is the passage-way from spiritual thirst to spiritual refreshing.[4]

JAMES H. MCCONKEY IN *PRAYER*

ENJOY HIS PRESENCE

Take some time now to think about your own view of prayer. How does what you have learned today affect how you will pray? How can you carry what you have learned today into your everyday life?

REST IN HIS LOVE

"Don't fret or worry. Instead of worrying, pray. Let petitions and praises shape your worries into prayers, letting God know your concerns. Before you know it, a sense of God's wholeness, everything coming together for good, will come and settle you down. It's wonderful what happens when Christ displaces worry at the center of your life" (Philippians 4:6-7, MSG).

when you suffer

When Jesus saw His mother, and the disciple whom He loved standing nearby,
He said to His mother, "Woman, behold, your son!"
JOHN 19:26

Prepare Your Heart

What a life Mary, the mother of Jesus, experienced! There were many times when it was turned upside down. Probably her lowest moment came as she watched her son's crucifixion, as he suffered humiliation, torture, and death as a common criminal. Whenever you find yourself at the foot of the cross, you will experience pain and some kind of death—it may be the death of a dream or a severe loss. One thing you must know: Your response to suffering may be your greatest work according to heaven. That is how it is in the economy of God.

We have the idea that our greatest ministry consists of the things we do, such as Bible studies, preaching, and discipleship. But Paul wrote,

Therefore we do not lose heart, but though our outer man is decaying, yet our inner man is being renewed day by day. For momentary, light affliction is producing for us an eternal weight of glory far beyond all comparison, while we look not at the things which are seen, but at the things which are not seen; for the things which are seen are temporal, but the things which are not seen are eternal. (2 Corinthians 4:16-18)

Your claim to fame in eternity may be your faith victory in one circumstance. Such was true for Job. It was also true for Jesus. The name that Jesus is known by in heaven is Lamb of God. The focus is on His sacrifice for our sins. Think about the ramifications of this in your own life. It means that no suffering is wasted. The suffering of Mary did not go unnoticed by Jesus while He was on the cross. He provided for her even in His own dark hour. Today you will have the opportunity to look at this powerful moment.

Turn now to Psalm 37 as you ask God to prepare your heart to hear Him speak in His Word today. What is your most significant insight from this psalm?

READ AND STUDY GOD'S WORD

1. Read John 19:14-30. What must this time have been like for Mary?

2. Something happened that changed sorrow to joy in the lives of those who loved Jesus. Turn to Mark 16:1-20. How do you think Jesus' resurrection affected Mary?

3. As he described the Jerusalem church in the book of Acts, Luke made a point of mentioning Mary's faith. What do you learn about her in Acts 1:14?

4. Jesus was not only Mary's great treasure in life, He is yours as well. Look at the following verses and record why He is your treasure in life. Personalize your insights as much as possible.

   John 1:1-5,9,12-14,17

   2 Corinthians 4:6-11

Ephesians 1:3-14

Colossians 1:12-20

ADORE GOD IN PRAYER

O God my Father, to you nothing is small and nothing great; the ages are as sands on the shore and nations as drops in the bucket. Help me to look not at this affliction, which is but for a moment, but to the far exceeding and eternal weight of glory.[1]

F. B. MEYER IN *DAILY PRAYERS*

YIELD YOURSELF TO GOD

Our hope is for a far more exceeding and eternal weight of glory. Because of this hope, we are enabled to suffer. By this hope, present sufferings are paled into nothingness by contrast. And for this hope, we are made willing to suffer for Christ. . . . Our afflictions whatever they are, whether pain, trouble, disappointment or illness, contribute to eternal glory. They are not the cause, but in the purpose of God He uses these to compensate us by grace with greater glory. By our sufferings for Him we are perfected. We might rightfully say that all things work together for good to them that love God. Moreover, our afflictions are very light in comparison with the weight of glory of the heavenlies, of eternity. Afflictions are momentary, passing, transient. They belong to time. The glory, which means the image of the Lord Jesus Christ, will be eternal. Our afflictions are in time, that is, they spread thin from one minute to the next minute, from one second to the next second, and we are thus able to bear them. If ten years of constant pain were rolled into one moment it would be unendurable because of the weight, but when we consider innumerable lifetimes of glory rolled into a moment or a present experience called eternity we begin to understand the contrast. Thus the glory is beyond measure. It exceeds all comparison and yet it is directly contingent upon the measure of affliction which we have endured for the sake of Christ in this world. This hope makes us willing to suffer for Christ's sake. . . . Far too many of us have our joys and our sorrows connected with the external, material, sensuous things of life. The practice of focusing one's vision spiritually upon the unseen in life, character, salvation and glory will remove the sting from present affliction.[2]

HAROLD J. OCKENGA IN *THE COMFORT OF GOD*

My Father's way may twist and turn,
My heart may throb and ache,
But in my soul I'm glad I know,
He maketh no mistake.

My cherished plans may go astray,
My hopes may fade away,
But still I'll trust my Lord to lead
For He doth know the way.

Tho' night be dark and it may seem
That day will never break;
I'll pin my faith, my all in Him,
He maketh no mistake.

There's so much now I cannot see,
My eyesight's far too dim;
But come what may, I'll simply trust
And leave it all to Him.

For by and by the mist will lift
And plain it all He'll make.
Through all the way, tho' dark to me,
He made not one mistake.[3]

A. M. OVERTON

ENJOY HIS PRESENCE
What is your favorite truth about Jesus today?

Why is He your great treasure?

How does knowing He is your great treasure help you in times of suffering?

REST IN HIS LOVE

"The Word became flesh and made his dwelling among us. We have seen his glory, the glory of the One and Only, who came from the Father, full of grace and truth" (John 1:14, NIV).

DEAR FRIEND,

The next two days are your opportunity to review what you have learned this week. You may wish to write your thoughts in your Journal. As you think about what you have learned about finding your treasure in life, write:

Your most significant insight:

Your favorite quote:

Your favorite verse:

Have you learned, like Mary, to treasure up the ways, works, and words of the Lord? If so, your heart will dance with the Lord. Close your time this week by thinking about these words of Donald Whitney in *Spiritual Disciplines for the Christian Life*:

Let's define meditation as deep thinking on the truths and spiritual realities revealed in Scripture for the purposes of understanding, application, and prayer. Meditation goes beyond hearing, reading, studying, and even memorizing as a means of taking in God's Word. A simple analogy would be a cup of tea. You are the cup of hot water and the intake of Scripture is represented by the tea bag. Hearing God's Word is like one dip of the tea bag into the cup. Some of the tea's flavor is absorbed by the water, but not as much as would occur with a more thorough soaking of the bag. In this analogy, reading, studying, and memorizing God's Word are represented by additional plunges of the tea bag into the cup. The more frequently the tea enters the water, the more effect it has. Meditation, however, is like immersing the bag completely and letting it steep until all the rich tea flavor has been extracted and the hot water is thoroughly tinctured reddish brown. . . . Meditation opens the soil of the soul and lets the water of God's Word percolate in deeply.[1]

hearts forever captivated

week
six

THE WOMEN AT BETHANY

the quiet place

And He left them and went out of the city to Bethany, and spent the night there.
MATTHEW 21:17

Prepare Your Heart

Where do you go when you need to take a break? It is that place where you can stop everything, take a deep breath of fresh air, slow down, and get some rest. There is no pressure to perform. If friends are with you, the conversation has no time constraints, and you are free to share from the heart. Everyone needs a place like this—a "quiet place."

Even Jesus had such a place. When He wanted to commune with His Father and intimate friends, He went to Bethany. Bethany is about two miles from Jerusalem on the far side of the Mount of Olives. It lies almost hidden in a small ravine. The ground is covered with fruit trees and waving grain. Jesus probably walked from Jerusalem, often at the end of a busy day, ascending the hill by a footpath that passes north of Gethsemane. His friends may have seen Him amid the trees or in the grassy field, in deep communion with the Father. He had good friends in Bethany—Mary, Martha, and Lazarus—who were captivated by a desire for intimacy with Him.

Everyone needs a Bethany. You need somewhere to be quiet, to have long, luxurious hours in fellowship with your Lord and with good friends. It is here that Jesus your Lord will captivate your heart. Your gaze will be fixed forever on His face. Here your heart will turn to God in such a way that you will never want to leave. These times will carry you through life's challenges. This is where you learn how to dance with the Lord.

Where is your Bethany? It is the place where Jesus is. Any place can be a Bethany if you will slow down and draw near to the Lord there. Today, will you draw near to God that He may draw near to you?

Turn to Psalm 132 and meditate on the words of David. Record your most significant observations.

Read and Study God's Word

1. Bethany was a special place for Jesus. Look at the following verses and record your insights related to the time Jesus spent in Bethany. Why did He go there? What events preceded His times in Bethany or occurred at Bethany?

Matthew 21:12-17

Matthew 26:1-13

Mark 11:1-11

John 11:1-46

Luke 24:50-53

2. Describe the place that would be your ideal quiet place.

3. Think of a time when you were in a quiet place and had memorable fellowship with the Lord. What was most significant about that time?

4. Think of a time when you were in a quiet place and had memorable fellowship with good friends. What is your favorite remembrance of that time?

Adore God in Prayer

O God, I have tasted Thy goodness, and it has both satisfied me and made me thirsty for more. I am painfully conscious of my need of further grace. I am ashamed of my lack of desire. O God, the Triune God, I want to want Thee; I long to be filled with longing; I thirst to be made more thirsty still. Show me Thy glory, I pray Thee, that so I may know Thee indeed. Begin in mercy a new work of love within me. Say to my soul, *Rise up, my love, my fair one, and come away*. Then give me grace to rise and follow Thee up from this misty lowland where I have wandered so long. In Jesus' name. Amen.[1]

A. W. Tozer in *The Pursuit of God*

Yield Yourself to God

How pleasing are all the associations that cluster around [Bethany]! Perhaps there was no scene in the Holy Land which afforded us more unmingled enjoyment: we even fancied that the curse that everywhere rests so visibly upon the land had fallen more lightly here. In point of situation, nothing could have come up more completely to our previous imagination of the place to which Jesus delighted to retire at evening, from the bustle of the city, and the vexations of the unbelieving multitudes—sometimes traversing the road by which we had come, and perhaps oftener still coming up the face of the hill by the footpath that passes on the north of Gethsemane. What a peaceful scene! Amidst these trees, or in that grassy field, he may often have been seen in deep communion with the Father. And in sight of this verdant spot it was that he took his last farewell of the disciples, and went upward to resume the deep, unbroken fellowship of *his God, and our God*, uttering blessings even at the moment when he began to be parted from them.[2]

Robert Murray McCheyne in *Bethany*

Even when we are not called to the monastic life, or do not have the physical constitution to survive the rigors of the desert, we are still responsible for our own solitude. Precisely because our secular milieu offers us so few spiritual disciplines, we have to develop our own. We have, indeed, to fashion our own desert where we can withdraw every day, shake off our compulsions, and dwell in the gentle healing presence of our Lord. . . . The very first thing we need to do is set apart a time and a place to be with God and him alone.[3]

HENRI NOUWEN IN THE WAY OF THE HEART

Will you find a quiet place where you can retreat with the Lord? Look at your schedule for the next month. When can you take some extended time just to be alone with the Lord? Where is your Bethany, that place of quiet and communion with Him?

ENJOY HIS PRESENCE

> Oh, for a closer walk with God,
> A calm and heavenly frame,
> A light to shine upon the road
> That leads me to the Lamb!
>
> Where is the blessedness I knew,
> When first I saw the Lord?
> Where is the soul-refreshing view
> Of Jesus and His Word?
>
> What peaceful hours I once enjoyed!
> How sweet their memory still!
> But they have left an aching void
> The world can never fill.

WILLIAM COWPER

REST IN HIS LOVE

"Come with me by yourselves to a quiet place and get some rest" (Mark 6:31, NIV).

sitting at His feet

She had a sister called Mary, who was seated at the Lord's feet, listening to His word.
LUKE 10:39

Prepare Your Heart

How do you develop a heart that is forever captivated by the Lord? All it takes is time with Him, listening to what He says. It's simple, but very few do it. Lots of people talk about spending time with the Lord. You can read books about it. You can attend conferences on it. Those things will not give you a heart that is captivated by the Lord. Only one thing will fix your heart on Him: that is, to stop, turn your gaze toward Him, sit at His feet, and listen to what He says.

Begin your time with the Lord today by meditating on the words of David in Psalm 19:7-14. Write a prayer below or in your Journal, asking the Lord to give you a heart that will sit at His feet, listening to His Word.

READ AND STUDY GOD'S WORD

1. One family in Bethany was especially close to Jesus: Mary, Martha, and Lazarus. The Bible includes a number of events involving these three people. One in particular highlights the actions of Mary and Martha. Today your goal is to look at the heart of Mary,

who loved her Lord with all her heart, soul, mind, and strength. Turn to Luke 10:38-42.
Describe what you see about Mary.

*Being with the Lord was most important to her
She wanted to hear what he had to say*

2. What does the Lord say about Mary's actions?

*The Lord is very important & she wanted
to be in his presence.*

3. David felt the same way as Mary in that desire to be in the Lord's presence. Read
Psalm 27:4-6. What did David want more than anything?

To sing to sing praises to the Lord

4. As you think about what the Lord said about Mary, how does this compare with your
own view about what is important in life? What is most important to you? What is the
Lord saying here to you?

ADORE GOD IN PRAYER

I have no word,
But neither hath the bird,
And it is heard;
My heart is singing, singing all day long
In quiet joy to Thee who art my Song.

For as Thy majesty,
So is Thy mercy,
So is Thy mercy,
My Lord and my God.

How intimate
Thy ways with those who wait

About Thy gate;
But who could show the fashion of such ways
In human words, and hymn them to Thy praise?

Too high for me,
Far shining mystery,
Too high to see;
But not too high to know, though out of reach
Of words to sing its gladness into speech.[1]

AMY CARMICHAEL IN *TOWARD JERUSALEM*

YIELD YOURSELF TO GOD

Christ is every man's contemporary. His presence and His power are offered to us in this time of mad activity and mechanical noises as certainly as to fishermen on the quiet lake of Galilee or to shepherds on the plains of Judea. The only condition is that we get still enough to hear His voice and that we believe and heed what we hear. . . . So today we must listen till our inner ears hear the words of God. When the Voice is heard it will not be as the excited shouting of the nervous world; rather it will be the reassuring call of One of whom it was said *He shall not strive, nor cry; neither shall any man hear his voice in the streets.* It cannot be heard in the street, but it may be heard plainly enough in the heart. And that is all that matters at last.[2]

A. W. TOZER IN GOD *TELLS THE MAN WHO CARES*

With us the training is of the *inner* ear. And its first training, after the early childhood stage is passed, must usually be through the eye. What God has spoken to others has been written down for us. We hear through our eyes. The eye opens the way to the inner ear. God spoke in His Word. He is still speaking in it and through it. The whole thought here is to get *to know* God. He reveals Himself in the word that comes from His own lips, and through His messengers' lips. He reveals Himself in His dealings with men. Every incident and experience of these pages is a mirror held up to God's face. In them we may come to see Him. This is studying the Bible not for the Bible's sake but for the purpose of knowing God. The object aimed at is not the Book but the God revealed in the Book.[3]

S. D. GORDON IN *QUIET TALKS ON PRAYER*

I want to make some simple suggestions for studying this Book [the Bible] so as to get to God through it. There will be the emphasis of doubling back on one's tracks here. For some of the things that should be said have already been said with a different setting. First there must be the *time* element. One must get at least a half hour daily when the mind is fresh. A tired mind does not readily *absorb*. This should be persisted in until there is a habitual spending of at least that much time daily over the Book, with a spirit at leisure from all else, so it can take in. Then the time should be given *to the Book itself*. If other books are consulted and read as they will be let that be after the reading of this Book. Let God talk to you direct, rather than through somebody else. Give Him first chance at your ears. This Book in the central place of your table, the others grouped about it. First time given to it. A third suggestion brings out the circle of this work. *Read prayerfully*. We learn how to pray by reading prayerfully. This Book does not reveal its sweets and strength to the keen mind merely, but to the Spirit enlightened mind. All the mental keenness possible, *with the bright light of the Spirit's illumination*—that is the open sesame. I have sometimes sought the meaning of some passage from a keen scholar who could explain the orientalisms, the fine philological distinctions, the most accurate translations, and all of that, who yet did not seem to know the simple spiritual meaning of the words being discussed. And I have asked the same question of some old saint of God, who did not know Hebrew from a hen's tracks, but who seemed to sense at once the deep spiritual truth taught. The more knowledge, the keener the mind, the better *if* illumined by the Spirit that inspired these writings. There is a fourth word to put in here. We must read *thoughtfully*. Thoughtfulness is in danger of being a lost art. Newspapers are so numerous, and literature so abundant, that we are becoming a bright, but a *not thoughtful* people. Often the stream is very wide but has no depth. Fight shallowness. Insist on reading thoughtfully. A very suggestive word in the Bible for this is "meditate." Run through and pick out this word with its variations. The word underneath that English word means to mutter, as though a man were repeating something over and over again, as he turned it over in his mind. We have another word, with the same meaning, not much used now—ruminate. We call the cow a ruminant because she chews the cud. She will spend hours chewing the cud, and then give us the rich milk and cream and butter which she has extracted from her food. That is the word here—ruminate. Chew the cud, if you would get the richest cream and butter here.

And it is remarkable how much chewing this Book of God will stand, in comparison with other books. You chew a while on Tennyson, or Browning, or Longfellow. And I am not belittling these noble writings. I have my own favourite among these men. But they do not yield the richest and yet richer cream found here. This Book of God has stood more of that sort of thing than any other, yet it is the freshest book to be found to-day. You read a passage over the two hundredth time and some new fine bit of meaning comes that you had not suspected to be there. There is a fifth suggestion, that is easier to make than to follow. Read *obediently*. As the truth appeals to your conscience let it change your habit and life.[4]

S. D. GORDON IN *QUIET TALKS ON PRAYER*

ENJOY HIS PRESENCE

Upon Thy Word I rest
Each pilgrim day.
This golden staff is best
For all the way.
What Jesus Christ hath spoken,
Cannot be broken!

Upon Thy Word I rest;
So strong, so sure,
So full of comfort blest,
So sweet, so pure:
The charter of salvation
Faith's broad foundation.

Upon Thy Word I stand: That cannot lie.
Christ seals it in my hand. He cannot lie.
Thy Word that faileth never: Abiding ever.

FRANCES RIDLEY HAVERGAL

Will you resolve to choose that one thing in life and be a Mary who sits at the feet of the Lord, listening to His Word? What is your most significant insight in your time with the Lord today, and how will you apply what you have learned to your life? Record your thoughts in your Journal.

REST IN HIS LOVE

"'If anyone has ears to hear, let him hear.' And He was saying to them, 'Take care what you listen to'" (Mark 4:23-24).

the reluctant disciple

But Martha was distracted with all her preparations.

LUKE 10:40

Prepare Your Heart

The event in Luke 10:38-42 has confused many readers. The text tells us that Martha was "distracted." Jesus applauded Mary's behavior and encouraged Martha not to be "worried and bothered" about so many things. The point of the story involves the priorities of a disciple. Without understanding the culture of the day, one might miss that point.

In those days, people sat on chairs or reclined on couches for meals. Disciples sat at the feet of their teachers to learn. The word *disciple* is *mathetes* in the original, literally, "one who learns." A disciple was one who adopted the philosophy, practices, and way of life of the teacher. In those days, this role was not open to women. A woman assuming the position of a disciple would shock Hebrew men. Yet Mary sat at Jesus' feet as a disciple, soaking in her Master's teaching. This was radical behavior. The question for you today is this: Are you a radical disciple or a reluctant disciple? This choice determines whether your heart will be forever captivated with the Lord Jesus Christ.

READ AND STUDY GOD'S WORD

1. Read Luke 10:38-42, focusing on Martha. What was she doing?

Serving

In Luke 10:40 we see that Martha was "distracted with all her preparations." The Greek word translated *distracted* means to be drawn in different directions, to be pulled or dragged away. Martha was dragged away by her preparations for all the guests in her house. Finally, she went to the Lord and complained. She probably expected that He would agree that Mary should be helping her with all the preparations. But the Lord's ways are not our ways, are they? How did the Lord answer Martha? With love, care, and concern—and a challenge.

2. What did the Lord say to Martha, and how did He say it? Record your insight about how the Lord related to Martha.

First, Jesus said, "Martha, Martha." The repetition of her name showed His love. While Martha may have been distracted, she had not escaped the attention and gaze of Jesus. He saw everything. But what He saw was not what others saw. "Man looks at the outward appearance, but the LORD looks at the heart" (1 Samuel 16:7, NIV). Jesus saw all the way into Martha's heart. He saw beyond her abilities and her gifts of hospitality, and reached her point of need. He first addressed her condition, and then gave her His challenge. About her condition He said, "You are worried and bothered about so many things."

Jesus was talking about priorities: the priorities of a disciple. Martha's priorities were "many things." These many things could be summed up in one word: service. These many things were causing her to be agitated and distracted.

3. What are the "many things" that can distract a believer from being a radical disciple for Christ?

4. Have you ever been distracted from your commitment to Christ? If so, describe that time.

Then Jesus challenged Martha. He said Mary had chosen what was better, and it would not be taken away from her. This word translated as *chosen* is in the aorist middle tense, which means it is a non-continuous action. Mary had already made the decision about the primacy of the Lord in her life, but Martha had not yet made the same choice. The verb was *eklegomai*, which meant to choose for oneself in a way that didn't reject what was not chosen, but gave favor to what was chosen. This verb emphasized the relationship being established between the chooser and the chosen. Mary wasn't rejecting the importance of preparing a meal, being hospitable, and all the other traditional woman's work; but her priority was something else, and Jesus said her priority was the best. Not only was it the best, it also could never be taken from her.

We have choices each day. We can be reluctant disciples, distracted by the many things of life. Or we can be radical disciples and sit at the Lord's feet and listen to His Word.

5. What is your choice today? Will you be a radical or a reluctant disciple? Is there anything in your life that is distracting you from the Lord today?

6. As we fast-forward in Scripture to another time in Martha's life, we find that she did have a heart forever captivated, one that dances with the Lord. Turn to John 11:1-44. Record what you see about Martha and her heart for the Lord.

ADORE GOD IN PRAYER

Make the words of this powerful prayer your own. Live in them today and carry them with you throughout the day.

> O my Saviour, help me.
> I am so slow to learn, so prone to forget, so weak to climb;
> I am in the foothills when I should be on the heights;
> I am pained by my graceless heart,
> My prayerless days,
> My poverty of love,
> My sloth in the heavenly race,
> My sullied conscience,
> My wasted hours,
> My unspent opportunities,
> I am blind while light shines around me:
> Take the scales from my eyes,
> Grind to dust the evil heart of unbelief.
> Make it my chiefest joy to study thee,
> Meditate on thee,
> Gaze on thee,
> Sit like Mary at thy feet,

Lean like John on thy breast,
Appeal like Peter to thy love,
Count like Paul all things dung.
Give me increase and progress in grace so that there may be
More decision in my character,
More vigour in my purposes,
More elevation in my life,
More fervour in my devotion,
More constancy in my zeal.
As I have a position in the world,
Keep me from making the world my position;
May I never seek in the creature
What can be found only in the creator;
Let not faith cease from seeking thee until it vanishes into sight.
Ride forth in me, thou king of kings and lord of lords,
That I may live victoriously, and in victory attain my end.[1]

FROM *THE VALLEY OF VISION*

YIELD YOURSELF TO GOD

Are you a reluctant or a radical disciple? Are you distracted or determined to follow the Lord Jesus Christ? Write a prayer of commitment to the Lord in your Journal today.

ENJOY HIS PRESENCE

Close your time with the Lord by meditating on the words of this hymn by Frances Ridley Havergal:

Take my life, and let it be
consecrated, Lord, to thee.
Take my moments and my days;
let them flow in ceaseless praise.
Take my hands, and let them move
at the impulse of thy love.
Take my feet, and let them be
swift and beautiful for thee.

Take my voice, and let me sing
always, only, for my King.
Take my lips, and let them be
filled with messages from thee.

Take my silver and my gold;
not a mite would I withhold.
Take my intellect, and use
every power as thou shalt choose.

Take my will, and make it thine;
it shall be no longer mine.
Take my heart, it is thine own;
it shall be thy royal throne.
Take my love, my Lord, I pour
at thy feet its treasure-store.
Take myself, and I will be
ever, only, all for thee.

REST IN HIS LOVE

"Therefore, I urge you, brothers, in view of God's mercy, to offer your bodies as living sacrifices, holy and pleasing to God—this is your spiritual act of worship. Do not conform any longer to the pattern of this world, but be transformed by the renewing of your mind. Then you will be able to test and approve what God's will is—his good, pleasing and perfect will" (Romans 12:1-2, NIV).

extravagant love

While He was in Bethany at the home of Simon the leper, and reclining at the table, there came a woman with an alabaster vial of very costly perfume of pure nard; and she broke the vial and poured it over His head.

MARK 14:3

Prepare Your Heart

Hearts forever captivated with the Lord Jesus Christ express their love to Him in extravagant ways. *Extravagance* means "above and beyond." It means you go the extra mile for Him. Your life is sold out to Jesus Christ. Wherever you go, whatever you do, it is *all for Him*. Your earthly vocation may be in an office, a restaurant, or outdoors. But your real vocation is to live for Him no matter what. Time alone with the Lord is not a question in extravagant love. It is a great joy and desire.

Robert Murray McCheyne lived in the early 1800s and had a heart forever captivated. He had an older brother who loved the Lord and was an example for him. Early on, he had no interest in God or spiritual things. But when his brother died, he realized his spiritual need and turned to God. He was greatly influenced by the books of such men of God as John Knox, David Brainerd, Richard Baxter, Jonathan Edwards, John Newton, and Charles Bridges. He worked closely with John and Andrew Bonar in Scotland. During that time, he lived in the written works of Jonathan Edwards and Samuel Rutherford. He fed himself so that he could feed others. Soon he became the pastor at St. John's in Dundee, Scotland.

He kept his daily schedule with great fervency, convinced that the morning hours belonged to God. He said, "I will not see the face of man till I have seen the face of God." It was prayer and praise that held his life and ministry together. His heart was filled with love for the Lord. As a result, he reached out to the poor, the sick, and the dying. Crowds flocked to hear him preach because he preached Christ and His love to them. Later in his life, he traveled to many different churches, touching others with the message of the love of Christ.

He also wrote many books, letters, and hymns during his brief stay on earth—just thirty years. He died of typhus on March 25, 1843.

This is just one man's story—one man who had an extravagant love for the Lord because of a heart that was captived. His name is not a household word, but he was famous with God and known intimately by the Lord. He had a heart that danced with the Lord.

So it is with you. Your name may not be a household word, but you can be famous with the Lord and extravagant in your love toward Him. Your intimacy with Him can be such that your heart is captivated. It begins in your own extravagance of time with Him. Will you say, along with Robert Murray McCheyne, "I will not see the face of man till I have seen the face of God"? When you do, that extravagant love will spill over into everything you do. Ask the Lord today to open your eyes, that you might behold wonderful things in His Word. You may wish to write a brief prayer to the Lord today, pouring out to Him all that is on your heart.

READ AND STUDY GOD'S WORD

1. Today you will see an exceptional example of extravagant love toward the Lord Jesus Christ. Turn to Mark 14:1-9. Describe what you see in this passage.

2. There is even more to the story. Turn to John 11:1-2. What additional details do you learn about the anointing?

3. What does this event tell you about Mary and her heart for the Lord?

4. Now read Luke 7:36-39. Many commentators think this was a separate event from the one recorded in Mark 14. If so, then here is another woman who could not help expressing her extravagant love for the Lord. What did she do?

5. What do you think prompted such an expression of love?

6. What does extravagant love look like? Read these verses and record your insights.
   Song of Solomon 1:3

   Pure

   Song of Solomon 2:3-4

   Sweet

   Song of Solomon 2:8-13

   Come follow me

7. The Bible says the church is the bride of Christ. The Lord longs for His people's love as a bridegroom longs to be loved by his bride. Because you are part of the church, that includes you. What do you learn from the following verses about the kind of love the Lord longs to give you and receive from you? If you are short on time, choose two passages and return later to look at the others.
   Isaiah 49:14-16

   Isaiah 54:4-8

   Luke 10:27

John 15:9

John 21:15-17

Ephesians 5:25-32

Revelation 21:1-2

8. What is your favorite insight today from God's Word?

ADORE GOD IN PRAYER

Today, as you talk with the Lord, turn to your Prayer Pages. What requests have you written there in the last few weeks? How is God answering your prayers? What new things are on your heart? Write these requests on your Prayer Pages. Then spend some time focusing your attention on the Lord. You might even turn to your Journal and write a letter to Him, telling Him what He has done that makes you love Him more. If you are in a difficult place right now, it might be helpful to turn to the Psalms and use them to help you talk with the Lord.

YIELD YOURSELF TO GOD

In approving Mary's action at Bethany, the Lord Jesus was laying down one thing as a basis of all service: that you pour out all you have, your very self, unto him; and if that should be all he allows you to do, that is enough. . . . The service of the Lord is not to be measured by tangible results. No, my friends, the Lord's first concern is with our position at his feet and our anointing of his head. Whatever we have as an *alabaster box*: the most precious thing, the thing dearest in the world to us—yes, let me say it, the *outflow from us of a life that is produced by the very Cross itself*—we give that all up to the Lord. To some, even of those who should understand, it seems a waste; but that is what he seeks above all. Often enough the giving to him will be in tireless service, but he reserves to himself the right to suspend the service for a time, in order to discover to us whether it is that, or himself, that holds us. . . . Oh, to be wasted! It is a blessed thing to be wasted for the Lord.[1]

WATCHMAN NEE IN *THE NORMAL CHRISTIAN LIFE*

When is bridal love for Jesus set aflame? Your bridal love will be the sooner set aflame the more you behold the Bridegroom Jesus, the more you meditate on Him, the more your heart converses with Him, and your tongue declares who He is. . . . Your bridal love will be deepened at every fresh encounter with your Bridegroom, as you converse with Him and share with Him. Seek frequent encounters with Jesus. The more you use every possible free moment for prayer, the more your love will grow. . . . Your bridal love will be set aflame when you do everything together with Jesus all day long. Do the smallest and most ordinary things with Him. Do the seemingly senseless things with Him. Everything you do with Him will inspire a new and precious love for Him, a constant love which will be evident in everyday life. . . . Your bridal love will be deepened if you do everything with the words: *For You!* Thus you will devote your love to His difficult tasks. . . . Your bridal love will be set aflame when you lie at the feet of the Crucified One, the Man of Sorrows, in repentance. A lack of repentance quenches the flame of love; repentance fans it. Repentance is fuel for love's fire; makes it burn brightly. . . . Only eyes which weep for sin have been opened and can really see Jesus in His beauty. If your eyes are dry, you may be able to speak much about Him, but you will not see Him with your heart and really love Him. . . . Your bridal love will be deepened when you are filled with the thought of the coming of Jesus, when you live for His second coming. . . . Expect Him! Watch for Him daily—for daily He draws near. But also wait for Him to come and take you home when your life draws towards its end. Then He will embrace you, and you will see Him face to face. . . . Your bridal love will be set aflame as you speak His name. The more a bride utters her Bridegroom's name, the more ardent her love will be. . . . Seek, then, times of utter quietness when no one can disturb you, when everything around you is silent, when you are not distracted by anything else, when you can give yourself to Jesus completely; when you are all His. Believe that He will draw close to you. Believe that He is there, that He will speak to your heart. Only he who dares to go aside, and dares to pass through times of dryness will know the visitation of His love, and this will enhance the flame of love.[2]

BASILEA SCHLINK IN *MY ALL FOR HIM*

Believer, look back through all thine experience, and think of the way whereby the Lord thy God has led thee in the wilderness, and how He hath fed and clothed thee every day—how He hath borne with thine ill manners—how He hath put up with all thy murmurings, and all thy longings after the flesh-pots of Egypt—how He has opened the rock to supply thee, and fed thee with manna that came down from heaven. Think of how His grace has been sufficient for thee in all thy troubles—how His blood has been a pardon to thee in all thy sins—how His rod and His staff have comforted thee. When thou hast thus looked back upon the love of the Lord, then let faith survey His love in the future, for remember that Christ's covenant and blood have something more in them than the past. He who has loved thee and pardoned thee, shall never cease to love and pardon. He is Alpha, and He shall be Omega also: He is first, and He shall be last. Therefore, bethink thee, when thou shalt pass through the valley of the shadow of death, thou needest fear no evil, for He is with thee. When thou shalt stand in the cold floods of Jordan, thou needest not fear, for death cannot separate thee from His love; and when thou shalt come into the mysteries of eternity thou needest not tremble, "For I am persuaded, that neither death, nor life, nor angels, nor principalities, nor powers, nor things present, nor things to come, nor height, nor depth, nor any other creature, shall be able to separate us from the love of God, which is in Christ Jesus our Lord." Now, soul, is not thy love refreshed? Does not this make thee love Jesus? Doth not a flight through illimitable plains of the ether of love inflame thy heart and compel thee to delight thyself in the Lord thy God? Surely as we meditate on "the love of the Lord," our hearts burn within us, and we long to love Him more.[3]

CHARLES SPURGEON IN MORNING AND EVENING

ENJOY HIS PRESENCE

Do you love the Lord Jesus? What is that alabaster box of costly perfume that you can break and pour on the Lord Jesus today? Is there something He has called you to do today that you can do in His Name? Something, perhaps, to which you can attach the words "For You" as you do it? Will you say His name today and draw near in love, just to be with Him? How will you apply in your life what you have thought about today?

Close your time now by meditating on these words:

Alabaster Heart

Nothing to Thee can I bring,
Holding to Thy hand I cling.
No alabaster box have I
To break open and anoint Thee by.
I have only the heart Thou gave to me
To live, to love, to honor Thee.
Take it, my Lord, it is Thine own
Humbly, I lay it before Thy throne.[4]

CONNI HUDSON

REST IN HIS LOVE
"Do you love Me more than these?" (words of Jesus to Peter in John 21:15).

a view of the spectacular

While He was blessing them, He parted from them and was carried up into heaven.

LUKE 24:51

Prepare Your Heart

The heart that is forever captivated sees things that others cannot see. It has a view of heaven and a vision of the extraordinary. It experiences things that only God can do. A person with such a heart lives a supernatural lifestyle. He or she never gives up. Although circumstances appear hopeless, by faith the captivated heart knows that with God all things are possible. God has a plan and will carry it out.

Today you have one last day in Bethany, Jesus' favorite place. As you begin your time with the Lord, turn to Psalm 18:1-19. Notice all the things God can do and all He is. You may write your insights below.

READ AND STUDY GOD'S WORD

1. Bethany was the scene of at least two spectacular events. Of course, there were probably many other extraordinary things that happened because Jesus was there. When Jesus is present, you have the opportunity to catch a glimpse of the spectacular. Look at the

following passages of Scripture. Record what happened in each event and why this event was extraordinary.

John 11:1-46

Luke 24:50-53

2. How do you think these events affected those who lived in Bethany?

3. How can knowing God transform your life? Personalize your answers. For example, "I can experience His grace and compassion."

Isaiah 30:18-21

Jeremiah 32:17,27

Jeremiah 33:2-3

Daniel 11:32

1 Corinthians 2:9

4. Those who have a heart forever captivated view life with the eyes of faith. Look at the following verses. What do you learn about faith and its importance in your life? Again,

personalize your answers. For example, "Without faith it is impossible *for me* to please God" (Hebrews 11:6).

2 Corinthians 4:18

2 Corinthians 5:7

Hebrews 11:1-6

1 John 5:4

5. What is your most significant insight from God's Word today?

ADORE GOD IN PRAYER

As you talk with the Lord today, think about all that He has done in your life. Make today a day of thanksgiving and praise. Worship the Lord for who He is and what He has done on your behalf. You might even turn to Psalm 18 and use those words as a prayer to Him.

YIELD YOURSELF TO GOD

With most men you can determine pretty nearly how they will act in given circumstances; you can enumerate the influences at work, and their value. But you can never be sure in the case of the Christian, because his faith is making real much of which the world around takes no thought whatever. . . . Faith is not careless of time, but more mindful of eternity. Faith does not underrate the power of man, but she magnifies omnipotence. Faith is not callous of present pain, but she weighs it against future joy. Against ill-gotten gains, she puts eternal treasure; against human hate the recompense of reward; against the weariness of the course, the crown of amaranth; against the tears of winter sowing, the shoutings of the autumn sheaves; against the inconvenience of the tent, the permanent city. None of these men would have lived the noble lives they did, had it not been for the recompense of reward and the gleams given them of the golden city amid the sorrows and straits of their lives.[1]

F. B. MEYER IN THE WAY INTO THE HOLIEST

Actually, we cannot trust anyone further than we know him. So we must not only learn the facts involved, but ever more intimately come to know the One who presents and upholds them![2]

MILES J. STANFORD IN THE GREEN LETTERS

He hath said [Hebrews 13:5] . . . If we can only grasp these words by faith, we have an all-conquering weapon in our hand. What doubt will not be slain by this two-edged sword? What fear is there which shall not fall smitten with a deadly wound before this arrow from the bow of God's covenant? Will not the distresses of life and the pangs of death; will not the corruptions within, and the snares without; will not the trials from above, and the temptations from beneath, all seem but light afflictions, when we can hide ourselves beneath the bulwark of "He hath said"? Yes; whether for delight in our quietude, or for strength in our conflict, "He hath said" must be our daily resort. And this may teach us the extreme value of searching the Scriptures. There may be a promise in the Word which would exactly fit your case, but you may not know of it, and therefore you miss its comfort. You are like prisoners in a dungeon, and there may be one key in the bunch which would unlock the door, and you might be free; but if you will not look for it, you may remain a prisoner still, though liberty is so near at hand. There may be a potent medicine in the great pharmacopoeia of Scripture, and you may yet continue sick unless you will examine and search the Scriptures to discover what "He hath said." Should you not, besides reading the Bible, store your memories richly with the promises of God? You can recollect the sayings of great men; you treasure up the verses of renowned poets; ought you not to be profound in your knowledge of the words of God, so that you may be able to quote them readily when you would solve a difficulty, or overthrow a doubt? Since "He hath said" is the source of all wisdom, and the fountain of all comfort, let it dwell in you richly, as "A well of water, springing up unto everlasting life." So shall you grow healthy, strong, and happy in the divine life.[3]

CHARLES SPURGEON IN MORNING AND EVENING

ENJOY HIS PRESENCE

Close by singing or reading aloud this great hymn to the Lord. Fanny Crosby, who was blind during her stay on earth, wrote these words. She may have been blind according to earth, but she had keen spiritual vision.

To God be the glory, great things He has done;
So loved He the world that He gave us His Son,
Who yielded His life an atonement for sin,
And opened the life gate that all may go in.

Refrain:

Praise the Lord, praise the Lord,
Let the earth hear His voice!
Praise the Lord, praise the Lord,
Let the people rejoice!
O come to the Father, through Jesus the Son,
And give Him the glory, great things He has done.

O perfect redemption, the purchase of blood,
To every believer the promise of God;
The vilest offender who truly believes,
That moment from Jesus a pardon receives.

Refrain

Great things He has taught us, great things He has done,
And great our rejoicing through Jesus the Son;
But purer, and higher, and greater will be
Our wonder, our transport, when Jesus we see.

Refrain

REST IN HIS LOVE

"For we walk by faith, not by sight" (2 Corinthians 5:7).

DEAR FRIEND,

The next two days are your opportunity to review what you have learned this week. You may wish to write your thoughts and insights in your Journal. As you think about what you have learned about hearts that are forever captivated, write:

Your most significant insight:

Your favorite quote:

Your favorite verse:

Close this week by meditating on these words by Robert Murray McCheyne in Bethany:

Bethany is a sweet retired village, about two miles from Jerusalem, in a ravine at the back of the Mount of Olives. It is at this day embosomed in fig-trees, and almond-trees, and pomegranates. But it had a greater loveliness still in the eyes of Christ—it was *the town of Mary and her sister Martha*. Probably the worldly people in Jerusalem knew Bethany by its being the town of some rich Pharisee who had his country villa there—or some luxurious noble, who called the lands after his own name; but Jesus knew it only as *the town of Mary and her sister Martha*. Probably they lived in a humble cottage, under the shade of a fig-tree; but that cottage was dear to Christ. Often, as he came over the Mount of Olives and drew near, the light in that cottage window gladdened his heart. Often he sat beneath their fig-tree telling them the things of the kingdom of God. His Father loved that dwelling; for these were justified ones. And angels knew it well; for night and day they ministered there to three heirs of salvation. No wonder he called the place *the town of Mary and her sister Martha*. That was its name in heaven.

So is it still. When worldly people think of our town, they call it the town of some rich merchant—some leading man in public matters—some great politician, who makes a dash as a friend of the people; not the town of our Martha's and Mary's. Perhaps some poor garret where an eminent child of God dwells, gives this town its name and interest in the presence of Jesus.

Dear believers, how great the love of Christ is to you! He knows the town where you live — the house where you dwell — the room where you pray. Often he stands at the door — often he puts in his hand at the hole of the door: "I have graven thee on the palms of my hands: thy walls are continually before me." Like a bridegroom loving the place where his bride dwells, so Christ often says: There they dwell for whom I died. Learn to be like Christ in this. When a merchant looks at a map of the world, his eye turns to those places where his ships are sailing; when a soldier, he looks to the traces of ancient battle-fields and fortified towns; but a believer should be like Jesus — he should love the spots where believers dwell.[1]

May the Lord Jesus Christ look at your town and attach your name to it because of the time you and He spend together there. May you be known as one who has a heart that dances with Him. May He bless you richly as you continue on in this great adventure of knowing Him!

the radical disciple

week
seven

PAUL

in obscurity

I did not immediately consult with flesh and blood, nor did I go up to Jerusalem to those who were apostles before me; but I went away to Arabia.

GALATIANS 1:16-17

Prepare Your Heart

As you become intimate with the Lord, something profound happens. A revolutionary transformation occurs in your heart, a transformation that others can see. The world and the church can see the effects of intimacy with the Lord. It cannot be helped. When Jesus Christ is present, extraordinary things happen. Intimacy with the Lord results in radical discipleship.

What is a radical disciple? It is that person who will follow Jesus Christ no matter what. The radical disciple is sold out to Him. Nothing else can sway that person. The eyes, the heart, the mind, and the soul are fixed on Jesus. In perilous times, in successful times, in times of challenge—no matter where that person is—Jesus Christ is given free rein to live and move and work. It has been said, "Only one life will soon be past, only what's done for Christ will last." This is the description of the radical disciple.

A. W. Tozer said that a disciple is one who faces one direction only, has stopped looking back, and has no further plans of his own. It is amazing to see the radical disciple in action. Onlookers wonder how that person does what he or she does. Insiders know it is the Lord Jesus Christ in action in and through that person. One Person alone motivates that person: the Lord Jesus Christ. Not accolades, not applause, not success, but ever and only the Lord Jesus Christ. The eye is single and the way is clear to that one who is intimate with the Lord and who is on that road of radical discipleship, following Him wherever He goes. How can you become a radical disciple? Become intimate with the Lord.

When you think of a radical disciple, you cannot help thinking of Paul. F. F. Bruce called him "the apostle of the heart set free."[1] This week you will look at Paul's relationship with the Lord Jesus Christ, who won his heart one day on the road to Damascus. You will look at him in different situations of life so that you can see not only how intimacy makes itself known, but also how it is developed. When a heart is surrendered to Christ, then intimacy with the Lord is constantly developing in that primary journey of life, the pilgrimage of the heart.

The question for you this week is probably the most important of this study. Will you be a radical disciple, one that stands out among the crowd? The world desperately needs to see the Lord Jesus Christ in action. The need of the hour is for one man, one woman, who will step out of the pack and say no to the things of this world and yes to Jesus Christ. Instead of wasting time on useless playthings, you say yes to spending time with the Lord and listening to Him speak in His Word. Time is short. Eternity is forever. Why not make the most of the time the Lord gives you?

If Jesus Christ is the truth, then to live for anything else is to live for a lie. If you will know the truth, the truth will set you free. You will be free to fly, to soar. Living for Christ enables you to soar above circumstances and to live a life of meaning as you participate in the purposes of God.

Today as you begin your quiet time with the Lord, think about these words from 2 Chronicles 16:9, spoken to a king: "The eyes of the Lord move to and fro throughout the earth that He may strongly support those whose heart is completely His." What do those words mean to you today?

READ AND STUDY GOD'S WORD

Today you will see Paul in a time of obscurity. Everyone's pilgrimage with the Lord is unique, designed by the Lord Himself. Even though Paul was one of the most brilliant men of his time, Jesus drew him aside for a prolonged time of aloneness and obscurity. Every great saint of the Lord has been called aside for such a time. This usually happens more than once in a life. Why? Because these times are imperative if one would know deep intimacy with the Lord. Imagine a paragraph with no commas or periods. These obscure times are the punctuation marks in life, times of rest and renewal to relish the character and person of your Lord.

For some, these times are periods of frustration, of not understanding what God is doing. Such people strive against the way of the Lord instead of listening to His words: "Be still, and know that I am God" (Psalm 46:10, NIV). But the radical disciple can thrive in times of obscurity. He or she will press through despair and aloneness to see, with the eyes of faith, the Lord's face. Then that disciple can dance, really dance, with the Lord.

Your study of Paul begins with his initial meeting with Christ. Always remember: you do not find Christ; He finds you and calls you to Himself. So it was with Paul. Who was Paul? His Hebrew name was Saul, but when he focused his ministry on nonJews, he started using his Greek name, Paul. Acts 7:54–8:4 describes a turning point in the church's life: the stoning of Stephen and the beginning of persecution of those who followed Christ.

1. Read Acts 7:54–8:4. What role did Saul play in this situation? What do you learn about him as a person?

2. Read the following passages, in which Paul shares his own story. What do you observe about who Saul was and how he met the Lord Jesus Christ?

Acts 22:1-16

Galatians 1:13-14

3. What happened after Paul met Christ? Read the following verses and record your insights. You may wish to consult a Bible atlas or the maps in the back of your Bible in order to follow Paul's journeys.

Acts 22:17-21

Galatians 1:15–2:2

The Lord took Paul alone to Arabia. The fact that Paul did not immediately consult with flesh and blood means that he drew near to the Lord Jesus Christ. He may have gone to Arabia "for the purpose of contemplation and solitary communion with God, to deepen his repentance and fortify his soul with prayer; and then perhaps his steps were turned to those mountain heights by the Red Sea, which Moses and Elijah had trodden before him."[2] Paul likely also preached the gospel of Christ in Arabia. He probably could not contain himself.

It would make sense that he would commune with Christ for an extended period of time. He was one of the most learned men in the Old Testament Scriptures, but now he knew the Messiah who had fulfilled those Scriptures. Now it all made sense. It would take Paul a lifetime to realize the ramifications of what he now knew. So he took extended time with the Lord, reflecting on the Scriptures. This is apparent in the letters that he wrote throughout his life.

4. The times when one is called aside are good times of intimacy with the Lord. The obscure time is the time of revelation of truth. In the following passages of Scripture, what are some of the things the Lord showed Paul during that time of obscurity?

2 Corinthians 12:1-10

Galatians 1:1

Galatians 1:10-12

Ephesians 2:8-13

Ephesians 3

Ephesians 6:12

5. Describe in your own words what it means to be in a time of obscurity. How do you think a time of obscurity is different from other times in life?

6. Have you ever had a time of obscurity? If so, what did you learn during that time?

ADORE GOD IN PRAYER

> I prayed for strength, and then I lost awhile
> All sense of nearness, human and divine;
> The love I leaned on failed and pierced my heart,
> The hands I clung to loosed themselves from mine;
> But while I swayed, weak, trembling, and alone,
> The everlasting arms upheld my own.
> I prayed for light; the sun went down in clouds,
> The moon was darkened by a misty doubt,

The stars of heaven were dimmed by earthly fears,
And all my little candle flames burned out;
But while I sat in shadow, wrapped in night,
The face of Christ made all the darkness bright.
I prayed for peace and dreamed of restful ease,
A slumber dragged from pain, a hushed repose;
Above my head the skies were black with storm,
And fiercer grew the onslaught of my foes;
But while the battle raged, and wild winds blew,
I heard His voice and perfect peace I knew.
I thank Thee, Lord, Thou wert too wise to heed
My feeble prayers, and answer as I sought,
Since these rich gifts Thy bounty has bestowed
Have brought me more than all I asked or thought;
Giver of good, so answer each request
With Thine own giving, better than my best.[3]

ANNIE JOHNSON FLINT, AS QUOTED BY MRS. CHARLES COWMAN IN *STREAMS IN THE DESERT*

Turn to the Lord now and lay at His feet the things that burden your heart. Talk to Him about everything. Write your specific requests on your Prayer Pages so that you can see how He answers you in His time.

YIELD YOURSELF TO GOD

What intensity of interest must have gathered for [Paul] about Mount Sinai, which doubtless was the objective of his journey into Arabia! Moses and Elijah had been pupils before him in its majestic solitudes. As the apostle dwelt there, with unlimited opportunity for communion with God, his mind was turned in the direction of that massive system of thought which at once distinguishes his epistles and connects the New Testament with the Old. It is a profound discovery when God reveals his Son as resident in the believer's soul. That Christ is in each of us, if we be truly regenerated, is indubitable.[4]

F. B. MEYER IN *F. B MEYER DEVOTIONAL COMMENTARY*

After every time of exaltation we are brought down with a sudden rush into things as they are where it is neither beautiful nor poetic nor thrilling. The height of the mountaintop is measured by the drab drudgery of the valley; but it is in the valley that we have to live for the glory of God. We see His glory on the mount, but we never live for His glory there. It is in the sphere of humiliation that we find our true worth to

God, that is where our faithfulness is revealed. Most of us can do things if we are always at the heroic pitch because of the natural selfishness of our hearts, but God wants us at the drab commonplace pitch, where we live in the valley according to our personal relationship to Him.[5]

OSWALD CHAMBERS IN MY UTMOST FOR HIS HIGHEST

It seems that most believers have difficulty in realizing and facing up to the inexorable fact that God does not hurry in His development of our Christian life. He is working from and for eternity! So many feel that they are not making progress unless they are swiftly and constantly forging ahead. Now it is true that the new convert often begins and continues for some time at a fast rate. But this will not continue if there is to be healthy growth and ultimate maturity. God Himself will modify the pace.[6]

MILES STANFORD IN PRINCIPLES OF SPIRITUAL GROWTH

Are you mourning before God because you have not had an audible response? You will find that God has trusted you in the most intimate way possible, with an absolute silence, not of despair, but of pleasure, because He saw that you could stand a bigger revelation. If God has given you a silence, praise Him, He is bringing you into the great run of His purposes. The manifestation of the answer in time is a matter of God's sovereignty. Time is nothing to God.[7]

OSWALD CHAMBERS IN MY UTMOST FOR HIS HIGHEST

One important lesson to be learned from the experience of those men is that in training a man for a ministry, God does not shorten the training days, as we so often wish to do. For both Moses and Paul a prolonged period of solitude was an important ingredient in their preparation and a necessary part of the maturing process. Spiritual leadership does not always develop best in the limelight. There must be time for a future leader's secret transactions with God and for getting to know Him more intimately than do those he is being trained to lead. Because God is seeking quality in our lives, time is no object to Him.[8]

J. OSWALD SANDERS IN ENJOYING INTIMACY WITH GOD

ENJOY HIS PRESENCE

Have you learned this secret of the radical disciple? Do not be afraid of the "punctuation marks" in life when you have the opportunity to rest in His love. These times of obscurity are not useless. You are not being set aside on a shelf. Rather, they are God's invitation to go deeper with Him in intimacy.

God wants to develop something with you that cannot be shaken no matter what comes your way. The only way for this to happen is much time spent alone with Him. You must become accustomed to His presence and comfortable in companionship with Him alone. How does this happen? In obscurity: those times when there is no one to cheer you on— only the Lord. And it is only the Lord whom you need. He is the One who will always be there, and He is the One you will see face to face in eternity. He will be center stage in heaven, and He must become center stage in your life here and now. Draw near to Him now as you think about these things.

Will you write a prayer to Him expressing what has been prompted in your heart and mind today?

REST IN HIS LOVE
"The eyes of the LORD move to and fro throughout the earth that He may strongly support those whose hearts are completely His" (2 Chronicles 16:9).

in weakness and peril

Most gladly, therefore, I will rather boast about my weaknesses,
so that the power of Christ may dwell in me.
Therefore I am well content with weaknesses,
with insults, with distresses, with persecutions,
with difficulties, for Christ's sake;
for when I am weak, then I am strong.
2 CORINTHIANS 12:9-10

Prepare Your Heart

When does it become apparent that someone is a radical disciple of Jesus Christ? In adversity. If a waiter is walking along holding a tray high above his head, you cannot see what is on the tray unless it is tipped over. Similarly, the world never sees the true character of a person unless *the tray is tipped.* How does one become a radical disciple of Jesus Christ who will follow Him wherever He leads? Through adversity. According to James, trials test the faith of a Christian and produce endurance, making that person "perfect and complete, lacking in nothing" (James 1:4). Your response to adversity will determine whether you become all that God wants you to be. The hard times show how radical you are for Christ, and they also produce intimacy with Him, that you may embrace Him all the more. It is a win-win situation.

As you begin this time with the Lord, meditate on Psalm 73. What is most significant to you in this psalm today?

READ AND STUDY GOD'S WORD

1. What does a radical disciple do in times of trouble? Paul's words and actions reveal a heart that is intimate with the Lord Jesus. Look at the following verses and record your insights about Paul's response to adversity.

Romans 8:31-39

2 Corinthians 11:23-33

2 Corinthians 12:7-10

2 Corinthians 4:7-18

Philippians 4:11-13

2. How would you summarize Paul's attitude in weakness and troubles?

3. What aspect of Paul's attitude helps you the most in a difficult time?

ADORE GOD IN PRAYER

Thee will I love, my Strength, my Tower,
Thee will I love, my Joy, my Crown,
Thee will I love with all my power,
In all Thy works, and Thee alone;
Thee will I love, till the pure fire
Fill my whole soul with chaste desire.

Ah, why did I so late Thee know,
Thee, lovelier than the sons of men!
Ah, why did I no sooner go
To Thee, the only ease in pain!
Ashamed, I sigh, and inly mourn,
That I so late to Thee did turn.

I thank Thee, uncreated Sun,
That Thy bright beams on me have shined;
I thank Thee, who hast overthrown
My foes, and healed my wounded mind;
I thank Thee, whose enlivening voice
Bids my freed heart in Thee rejoice.

Uphold me in the doubtful race,
Nor suffer me again to stray;
Strengthen my feet with steady pace
Still to press forward in Thy way;
My soul and flesh, O Lord of might,
Fill, satiate, with Thy heavenly light.

Give to mine eyes refreshing tears,
Give to my heart chaste, hallowed fires,
Give to my soul, with filial fires,
The love that all heaven's host inspires;

That all my powers, with all their might,
In Thy sole glory may unite.

Thee will I love, my Joy, my Crown,
Thee will I love, my Lord, my God;
Thee will I love, beneath Thy frown,
Or smile, Thy sceptre, or Thy rod;
What though my flesh and heart decay,
Thee shall I love in endless day.[1]

JOHANN SCHEFFLER (1624–1677), TRANS. JOHN WESLEY (1703–1791)

YIELD YOURSELF TO GOD

Do you know, a dead level in a man's life would be his ruin? If he had nothing but prosperity, he would be ruined. A man can stand adversity better than prosperity. I know a
great many men who have become very prosperous, but I know few that haven't lost
all their piety, that haven't lost sight of that city eternal in the heavens, whose builder
and maker is God. Earthly things have drawn their heart's affections away from eternal
things. . . . I have an idea that we will thank God in eternity for our reverses and trials
more than for anything else. I believe John Bunyan thanked God for the Bedford Jail
more than anything that happened to him down here. I believe Paul thanked God for
the rods and stripes more than for anything else that happened to him. . . . Are you
passing through the waters? Don't get discouraged! You are an heir of glory, and if God
calls you to pass through deep waters, go on; He is with you. He was with Joseph when
he was cast into prison; they had to put the Almighty in with him. I had rather be in
prison with the Almighty than outside without Him. You needn't be afraid of prison
and, my dear friends, you needn't be afraid of the grave, you needn't be afraid of death.
Cheer up, child of God; the time of our redemption draweth near! We may have to suffer a little while, but when you think of the eternal weight of glory, you can afford to
suffer, can't you? I think we will be so ashamed of ourselves when we get to heaven, to
remember we ever spoke about our sufferings.[2]

D. L. MOODY IN MOODY'S LATEST SERMONS

So then, though we may not know what trials wait on any of us, we can believe that,
as the days in which Job wrestled with his dark maladies are the only days that make
him worth remembrance, and but for which his name had never been written in the
book of life, of the days through which we struggle, finding no way, but never losing
the light, will be the most significant we are called to live (Robert Collyer). Who does
not know that our most sorrowful days have been amongst our best? When the face is

wreathed in smiles and we trip lightly over meadows be-spangled with spring flowers, the heart is often running to waste. The soul which is always blithe and gay misses the deepest life. It has its reward, and it is satisfied to its measure, though that measure is a very scanty one. But the heart is dwarfed; and the nature, which is capable of the highest heights, the deepest depths, is undeveloped; and life presently burns down to its socket without having known the resonance of the deepest chords of joy. *Blessed are they that mourn*. Stars shine brightest in the long dark night of winter. The gentians show their fairest bloom amid almost inaccessible heights of snow and ice. God's promises seem to wait for the pressure of pain to trample out their richest juice as in a wine-press. Only those who have sorrowed know how tender is the *Man of Sorrows*.[3]

Mrs. Charles Cowman in Streams in the Desert

Enjoy His Presence

In times of weakness and difficulty, will you stand "strong in the Lord and in the strength of His might" (Ephesians 6:10)? As a radical disciple, your strength is in Christ. In Him you can "overwhelmingly conquer" (Romans 8:37). You may be weak, but He is strong. Will you rest in His strength and love today?

What is your most significant insight from your time with the Lord today? How will you apply it in your life?

Rest in His Love

"I have learned to be content in whatever circumstances I am. I know how to live in lowly circumstances and I know how to live in plenty. I have learned the secret, in all circumstances, of either getting a full meal or of going hungry, of living in plenty or being in want. I can do anything through Him who gives me strength" (Philippians 4:11-13, WMS).

in ministry

For I want you to know how great a struggle I have on your behalf and for those who are at Laodicea, and for all those who have not personally seen my face, that their hearts may be encouraged.

COLOSSIANS 2:1-2

Prepare Your Heart

It has been said that the world has yet to see what God can do in and through those whose lives are wholly yielded to Him. It is exciting to watch the Lord work in and through the life of a radical disciple, one whose heart is yielded to the Lord. One of the results of an intimate relationship with the Lord in a radical disciple is what the church calls "ministry." Ministry is *Jesus Christ in action*. When the Lord Jesus is in action, amazing things happen. It is as though a pebble is dropped in a clear pool. It creates a ripple that in turn creates another until the ripples reach far beyond that one little pebble.

In the late 1800s, a Sunday school teacher named Edward Kimball learned that he was going to die. Because he knew he had little time left, he set out to lead all of his Sunday school students to the Lord. He led one to the Lord in the back room of a store. That student's name was Dwight L. Moody. Moody went on to become a great evangelist.

One day Moody was preaching in Britain, and a teacher was moved by his message. She shared Moody's testimony with her students. Then she told her preacher that all of her students had given their lives to the Lord. That preacher's name was F. B. Meyer. The teacher's report moved Meyer to realize what it meant to be brokenhearted over sin and of the great need to point others to Christ.

Meyer came to America and preached at Moody's school in Northfield, Massachusetts. During his message he gave a heartfelt challenge: "If you're not willing to give up everything for Christ, are you willing to be made willing?" That remark moved the heart of a young preacher named J. Wilbur Chapman. He became a great evangelist during his time. When he returned to the pastorate, he turned over his ministry to the YMCA clerk who had been his advance man. His name was Billy Sunday.

Billy Sunday conducted a revival meeting in Charlotte, North Carolina. Out of that meeting a group of laymen formed a permanent organization to continue sharing the message of Christ in their city. Eight years later, in 1932, that group brought an evangelist named Mordecai Ham to their area to conduct citywide evangelistic meetings. One evening during one of the meetings, a lanky sixteen-year-old stepped out of the choir and gave his life to Jesus Christ. His name was Billy Graham. And the ripple effect continues.

Who knows the ripple effect that is occurring as a result of your relationship with the Lord? Will you be that radical disciple, yielded to Christ, with eyes fixed on Him? You will have such joy as you love others in His name.

READ AND STUDY GOD'S WORD

1. Paul had an incredible ministry. What a heart he had for the churches! And what an impact he had with his personal visits and his letters to the churches. He also took others with him who learned from him. Look at the following verses and record what you learn about Paul and his ministry. Notice his heart for the people and how he conducted himself as he ministered to the churches.

Acts 14:25-28

Acts 20:13-38

Romans 1:6-16

Romans 15:13–16:27

1 Corinthians 4:14-17

2 Corinthians 3:1-6

2 Corinthians 11:27-29

Colossians 2:1-6

2. Think about all you have read about Paul. In what ways did he minister to those around him?

3. How can you follow Paul's example in reaching out to those around you? What ministries has the Lord given you?

ADORE GOD IN PRAYER

Today, take some time to think about those in your life that are part of your ministry. It will include family, friends, coworkers, brothers and sisters in Christ at church, and many others. Bring each area of your ministry before the Lord, and ask Him to do a mighty work in and through you.

YIELD YOURSELF TO GOD

How largely his letters bulk in the make-up of the New Testament! They make a fourth part of the whole. And their importance must be measured not by length but by weight. Consider the precious treasures you are handling. The sublime chapter on love

(I Cor. 13); the matchless argument on justification (Rom. 4.5); the glorious exposition of the work of the Holy Spirit (Rom. 8); the triumphant resurrection hope (I Cor. 15); the tender unveiling of the love between Jesus and His own (Eph. 5)—what priceless treasures these are which the church owes first to the Holy Ghost, and next to the apostle Paul, acting as His organ and instrument. How many of the most precious and helpful passages in Scripture bear the mark of the tender, eager, fervent, and devout spirit of the apostle of the Gentiles.

The epistles marvelously reflect his personality. It has been said of one of the great painters that he was accustomed to mix his colors with blood drawn from a secret wound; and of Paul it may be said that he dipped his pen in the blood of his heart.

It is not too much to say that, humanly speaking, the gospel of Christ would never have taken such fast hold on the strong, practical, vigorous nations of the West, had it not been for these epistles. They are characterized by a virility, a logical order, a style of arguments, a definiteness of statement and phraseology, which are closely akin to our Western civilization. It is for this reason that Paul had been the contemporary of Western civilization through all the centuries. It was he who taught Augustine and inspired Luther. His thoughts and conceptions have been worked into the texture of the foremost minds of the Christian centuries. The seeds he scattered have borne fruit in the harvests of modern education, jurisprudence, liberty, and civilization.

Ah! it has been eloquently said, what does the world owe to this apostle; what has it owed to him; what will it owe: of pious pastors, zealous missionaries, eminent Christians, useful books, benevolent endowments, examples of faith, charity, purity, holiness? The whole human race will confess that there is no one to whom it proclaims with so much harmony, gratitude and love, as the name of the apostle Paul.[1]

F. B. MEYER IN *GREAT MEN OF THE BIBLE*, VOL. 2

ENJOY HIS PRESENCE

Think about the responsibility of ministry that Paul took on. He paid the price in time and energy to know the Lord and then encourage others in the Lord. He could have chosen to do something else with his time. Instead, he wrote those letters and visited those churches and spent time with others to disciple them in the ways of the Lord. Has the Lord put some-one in particular on your heart today? How can you minister to him or her? Is there an encouraging note or letter you could write, as Paul did to the churches? Or is there a phone call for you to make as an encouragement to someone else? How can you take what you have learned and apply it to your life today?

REST IN HIS LOVE

"Apart from such external things, there is the daily pressure on me of concern for all the churches" (2 Corinthians 11:28).

in controversy and conflict

And I, brethren, could not speak to you as to spiritual men,
but as to men of flesh, as to infants in Christ.
1 CORINTHIANS 3:1

Prepare Your Heart

As you walk with the Lord Jesus Christ, you will encounter things and people that threaten your peace, your joy, and your ministry. Controversies require the wisdom of the Lord. Conflicts require humility and surrender in your own heart so that you may respond with the love of Christ. In your human flesh, these things are seemingly impossible at times. However, in God's Spirit, you can move with grace when something difficult comes your way.

Today as you draw near to the Lord, meditate on the words of this hymn. If you know the melody, you may wish to sing it to the Lord.

When morning gilds the skies
my heart awakening cries:
May Jesus Christ be praised!
Alike at work and prayer,
to Jesus I repair:
May Jesus Christ be praised!

The night becomes as day
when from the heart we say:
May Jesus Christ be praised!
The powers of darkness fear
when this sweet chant they hear:
May Jesus Christ be praised!

Let all the earth around
ring joyous with the sound:
May Jesus Christ be praised!
In heaven's eternal bliss
the loveliest strain is this:
May Jesus Christ be praised!

Be this, while life is mine,
my canticle divine:
May Jesus Christ be praised!
Be this th' eternal song
through all the ages long:
May Jesus Christ be praised!

Katholisches Gesangbuch (from the German)

READ AND STUDY GOD'S WORD

1. Paul dealt with many conflicts. These included the controversy about law and grace, factions in the Corinthian church, the question of whether to include John Mark in his ministry team, and conflicts with various enemies. How did he deal with each of these conflicts? Record your insights as you look at each one.

Acts 13:5-13: the magician (and some mentions of John Mark)

Acts 15:1-31: the controversy over law and grace in the worldwide church

Galatians 2:11–3:6: the controversy over law and grace in the Galatian church

Acts 15:35-41: Paul and Barnabas part ways over the question of John Mark

Colossians 4:10; 2 Timothy 4:11: reconciliation with John Mark

Acts 19:8-20: evil in Ephesus

1 Corinthians 5:1-5: immorality in the church

1 Corinthians 3: factions in the Corinthian church

2. This has been an extensive study in God's Word as you have seen Paul dealing with controversies and difficulties. What you have really seen is *ministry*: Jesus Christ in action. You have seen an intimacy between Paul and the Lord as they cared deeply for the church. Paul's heart ached for the church—not for an institution, but for people. He desired to see them grow and be strong in the Lord. You could spend a lifetime looking

at all the ways he encouraged the church, even in the midst of much conflict. As you have looked at Paul and his ministry, what has stood out to you the most?

3. What has God laid on your heart that you can apply to your own ministry?

ADORE GOD IN PRAYER

Place all that is on your heart in the hands of the Lord today. Talk with Him, knowing that He is sitting there with you.

> O Savior, who goes after those who are lost until you find them, teach me to minister to the needs of others. May I compassionately regard those who do not know you and whose lives are one long outrage against your forbearing love. Give me something of your Shepherd compassion and longsuffering.[1]
>
> F. B. MEYER IN DAILY PRAYERS

YIELD YOURSELF TO GOD

Paul's position on the circumcision question was clearcut because he had thought it through; the Jerusalem leaders had not as yet had any occasion to think it through, and so their position was not so clearcut. The conversion of Cornelius, and even the ingathering of Gentile believers at Antioch, had been treated by them on an *ad hoc* basis. When, as a result of the current agitation, they were compelled to think it through, they reached the same conclusion as Paul, in so far as they came to agree that circumcision was not to be imposed on Gentile Christians. As Paul saw the new situation introduced by the coming of Christ, circumcision was no longer of any account. A man might be circumcised or uncircumcised: it made no difference in his relation to God. What Paul did oppose was the idea that, by submitting to circumcision as a religious obligation, a man could acquire merit in God's sight. . . . Paul was persuaded that the freedom of the Spirit was a more powerful incentive to the good life than all the ordinances or decrees in the world.[2]

F. F. Bruce in *Paul: Apostle of the Heart Set Free*

Satan doesn't bother very much with those who stay away from God. He does bother those who want to come close to God, because he knows that what the Bible promises is true: *Come near to God and he will come near to you* (James 4:8). And he doesn't want God to do that. Often the higher we go spiritually—that is, the closer we draw to God—the more we will have to bear what is unpleasant. Satan will put pressure on him. Jesus had admirers. There were some who liked what he did. But in the crunch, those in authority would not accept him. He was acceptable to most if he didn't go against anybody. But when he did (and to be faithful to the Father he had to), the pressure from those who were Satan's followers came down on him. If you are faithful to Christ, you may be pressured by Satan too. To obey Christ is to take up a cross and follow him. . . . But Christians who are faithful, who are hated for Christ's sake, though they are knocked down, don't stay down—they know that other people's opinions of them don't really matter. For the Christian, God's opinion counts. Remember: *For the Lord God is a sun and shield; the Lord bestows favor and honor; no good thing does he withhold from those whose walk is blameless* (Psalm 84:11). And if troubles come, don't worry about it; you know what is happening—God owns you; keep going. Hear what Scripture says about you: *The steps of good men are directed by the Lord. He delights in each step they take* (Psalm 37:23 TLB). Those words are for you.[3]

Roger C. Palms in *Enjoying the Closeness of God*

There are no dilemmas out of which you shall not be delivered if you live near to God, and your heart be kept warm with holy love. He goes not amiss who goes in the company of God. Like Enoch, walk with God, and you cannot mistake your road. You have infallible wisdom to direct you, immutable love to comfort you, and eternal power to defend you. *Jehovah*—mark the word—*Jehovah shall guide thee continually* (Isaiah 58:11).[4]

Charles Spurgeon in *Morning and Evening*

ENJOY HIS PRESENCE

Is there a conflict in your own life? How can you respond with the love of Christ in this present conflict?

REST IN HIS LOVE

"Whatever you do, do your work heartily, as for the Lord rather than for men" (Colossians 3:23).

in life

I do all things for the sake of the gospel, so that I may become a fellow partaker of it. Do you not know that those who run in a race all run, but only one receives the prize? Run in such a way that you may win.
1 CORINTHIANS 9:23-24

Prepare Your Heart

Radical disciples have a strong sense of their goal in life. They know in their heart what life is all about. They know what motivates them from day to day. And they are satisfied only with one thing: *knowing the Lord*. Only intimacy with the Lord has the power to drive them on in life. As they are close to the Lord, He gives them that goal that will be their focus throughout life.

The desire of Dr. Bill Bright with Campus Crusade for Christ is to see the Great Commission of Jesus Christ in Matthew 28:18-20 fulfilled. He signs his letters, "Yours for fulfilling the Great Commission in this generation." J. I. Packer's focus is helping others know God. Paul said, "I do all things for the sake of the gospel" (1 Corinthians 9:23). He had a reckless abandonment to the will of God and counted everything as loss compared to knowing Christ as his Lord.

Do you know what drives you? Do you know your goal? Do you have a verse that has become your life verse? These are things to think about as you continue on in your journey of intimacy with the Lord. They are imperative in the life of one who would be a radical disciple, willing to follow the Lord Jesus wherever He leads.

Turn to Psalm 27 and meditate on these words of David. Note his strong sense of his goal in life. Note what meant more to him than anything else.

READ AND STUDY GOD'S WORD

1. It's wonderful that Paul's many letters help us see his heart. Look at the following verses, and write your insights about Paul's goals, identity, resolves, statements of faith, and convictions in life.

1 Corinthians 2:1-2

1 Corinthians 9:19-27

Philippians 1:1

Philippians 1:18

Philippians 3:7-14

2 Timothy 1:8-12

2 Timothy 4:17-18

2. What statement do you most appreciate from Paul?

3. Intimacy with the Lord does not just happen. It begins with a resolve, a conviction, and a focus. It means arriving at an understanding of what life is all about. What is your commitment and resolve about intimacy with the Lord? Write out your desire and goals for your relationship with the Lord.

4. List any other goals and resolves you have as a result of walking with the Lord.

ADORE GOD IN PRAYER

Lord of all being, throned afar,
thy glory flames from sun and star;
Center and soul of every sphere,
Yet to each loving heart how near.

Sun of our life, Thy quickening ray
Sheds on our path the glow of day;
Star of our hope, thy softened light
Cheers the long watches of the night.

Our midnight is Thy smile withdrawn;
Our noontide is Thy gracious dawn;
Our rainbow arch, Thy mercy's sign;
All, save the clouds of sin, are Thine.

Lord of all life, below, above,
Whose light is truth whose warmth is love,
Before Thy ever blazing throne
We ask no luster of our own.

Grant us Thy truth to make us free,
And kindling hearts that burn for Thee,
Till all Thy living altars claim
One holy light, one heavenly flame.

OLIVER WENDELL HOLMES (1809–1894)

YIELD YOURSELF TO GOD

Paul was devoted to a Person not to a cause. He was absolutely Jesus Christ's, he saw nothing else, he lived for nothing else.[1]

OSWALD CHAMBERS IN MY UTMOST FOR HIS HIGHEST

I find the greatest thing in this world not so much where we stand, as in what direction we are moving. To reach the port of heaven, we must sail sometimes with the wind, and sometimes against it, but we sail, and not drift, nor lie at anchor.

OLIVER WENDELL HOLMES IN THE AUTOCRAT OF THE BREAKFAST TABLE

Though we do not hear much of it in this age of spineless religion, there is nevertheless much in the Bible about the place of moral determination in the service of the Lord. *Jacob vowed a vow*, and it was the beginning of a very wonderful life with God. The following years brought a great many vicissitudes, and Jacob did not always acquit himself like a true man of God, but his early determination kept him on course, and he came through victorious at last. . . . Paul *determined not to know anything among you, save Jesus Christ, and Him crucified*, and in that determined spirit ignored the learned philosophers, preached a gospel that was accounted foolishness and earned himself a reputation for ignorance, though he was easily the greatest brain of his generation. . . . In the diaries of some of God's greatest saints will be found vows and solemn pledges made in moments of great grace when the presence of God was so real and so wonderful that the reverent worshiper felt he dared to say anything, to make any promise, with the full assurance that God would enable him to carry out his holy intention. . . . Let us, then, set our sails in the will of God. If we do this we will certainly find ourselves moving in the right direction, no matter which way the wind blows.[2]

A. W. TOZER IN THE SET OF THE SAIL

Enjoy His Presence

Do you detect that resolve in Paul that never gives up? You must have that as well. The Lord was Paul's motivation for everything he did. Therefore, he walked with purpose no matter where Jesus led him or what happened along the way. Will you, as you walk in intimacy with the Lord, write out your convictions and resolves that come to your heart? Review them often, and do not be afraid to pour them out to the Lord.

What is your most significant insight today? How can you carry what you have learned with you throughout the day? How will it make a difference in your life today?

One ship drives east and another drives west
with the selfsame winds that blow;
'tis the set of the sails
and not the gales
which tells us the way to go.[3]

Ella Wheeler Wilcox in "The Wind of Fate"

Rest in His Love

"But all those things that I might count as profit I now reckon as loss for Christ's sake. Not only those things; I reckon everything as complete loss for the sake of what is so much more valuable, the knowledge of Christ Jesus my Lord. For his sake I have thrown everything away; I consider it all as mere garbage, so that I may gain Christ and be completely united with him" (Philippians 3:7-9, TEV).

DEAR FRIEND,

The next two days are your opportunity to review what you have learned this week. You may wish to write your thoughts and insights in your Journal. As you think about what you have learned about Paul and being a radical disciple, record:

Your most significant insight:

Your favorite quote:

Your favorite verse:

How would you describe a radical disciple?

Close this week by meditating on these words:

Paul strikes us as a man possessed of uncommon strength of will, not easily to be turned aside from the path which he believed it to be his duty to follow. Since the risen Lord had called him to be his apostle to the Gentiles, he had no option but to obey him. He obeyed him right gladly, with utter heart-devotion: the love of Christ constrained him. But even if he had felt otherwise about it, he had no option in the matter. He had been conscripted into this service. Never, to be sure, was there a more willing conscript, but he knew himself to be under authority. In other respects he might be allowed freedom of choice: not in this.[1]

F. F. BRUCE IN *PAUL: APOSTLE OF THE HEART SET FREE*

We should follow our Lord as unhesitatingly as sheep follow their shepherd, for *He has a right to lead us wherever He pleases*. We are not our own, we are bought with a price — let us recognize the rights of the redeeming blood. The soldier follows his captain, the servant obeys his master, much more must we follow our Redeemer, to whom we are a purchased possession. . . . Wherever Jesus may lead us, *He goes before us*. If we know not where we go, we know *with whom* we go. With such a companion, who will dread the perils of the road? The journey may be long, but His everlasting arms will carry us to the end. . . . Let us put full trust in our Leader, since we know that, come prosperity or adversity, sickness or health, popularity or contempt, his purpose shall be worked out, and that purpose shall be pure, unmingled good to every heir of mercy. We shall find it sweet to go up the bleak side of the hill with Christ, and when rain and snow blow into our faces, His dear love will make us far more blest than those who sit at home and warm their hands at the world's fire. To the top of Amana, to the dens of lions, or to the hills of leopards, we will follow our Beloved Precious Jesus, draw us, and we will run after Thee.[2]

CHARLES SPURGEON IN *MORNING AND EVENING*

the disciple Jesus loved

week
eight

JOHN

enjoy a privileged intimacy

There was reclining on Jesus' bosom one of His disciples, whom Jesus loved.
JOHN 13:23

Prepare Your Heart

A place is waiting for you—it's open to one who is willing to get close. It is the place of intimacy—leaning into the safe and secure arms of the Lord Jesus. He is waiting. He never holds His own at a distance but instead desires to embrace you. He wants to lavish his unconditional love on you.

Jesus said, "Jerusalem, Jerusalem, who kills the prophets and stones those who are sent to her! How often I wanted to gather your children together, the way a hen gathers her chicks under her wings, and you were unwilling" (Matthew 23:37). Why doesn't everyone enjoy such a privileged intimacy? Most are unwilling. Most stand at a distance, holding the Lord at least at arm's length. They do this because they are afraid to be so vulnerable and to be known so completely. You are exposing to Jesus the *you* that can be touched and moved and changed.

There are no shortcuts, however, to intimacy with the Lord. James said, "Draw near to God and He will draw near to you" (James 4:8). Jesus said, "Behold, I stand at the door and knock; if anyone hears My voice and opens the door, I will come in to him and will dine with him, and he with Me" (Revelation 3:20). Jesus wants you near to Him. In fact, some of the last words He gave to His disciples were, "Remain in me and I will remain in you" (John 15:4, NIV).

It is fitting on this last week of study that we look at one who enjoyed this great privilege of intimacy with the Lord Jesus Christ. His name: John. When John wrote his gospel to tell others about Jesus, he called himself the disciple "whom Jesus loved." John's one claim was that Jesus loved him. The question for you this week is: Can you say that you are a disciple whom Jesus loves? What would it take to be able to say that?

First, have you answered His call of discipleship: "Follow Me, and I will make you fishers of men" (Matthew 4:19)? And then, are you enjoying an intimate relationship with your Lord? Do you come close to Him? Do you lean on Him throughout the day? Is everything you say and do dependent on Him? Do you know His love in your own life? The invitation is extended to you: "Draw near to God and He will draw near to you" (James 4:8). Then you will be the one who has a heart that dances. This week we will look at what is true about one who is enjoying that privileged intimacy with the Lord.

As you begin your quiet times this week, write a prayer asking the Lord to open your heart and enable you to draw close to Him and stay there, leaning on Him throughout the day.

READ AND STUDY GOD'S WORD

1. Who was John, the beloved disciple? Look at the following verses and record what you learn about him.

Matthew 4:18-22; Mark 1:19-20

Mark 3:13-17

Matthew 17:1-3

Mark 5:35-43

Mark 10:35-45

Mark 13:1-4

Matthew 26:36-38

Acts 1:13-14

Acts 3:1-4

2. How intimate was John with Jesus? Look at John 13:1-32. Imagine that you are sitting in this room with Jesus. Keep in mind that the disciple "whom Jesus loved" is John. Describe what you notice about the relationship John had with Jesus.

ADORE GOD IN PRAYER

Will you lean on Jesus today? Will you converse with Him as you would someone with whom you are intimate? Tell Him everything that is on your heart today. Ask Him to open your heart to see and know Him more. Be sure to write any specific requests on your Prayer Pages so you can know He is answering your prayers.

YIELD YOURSELF TO GOD

Jesus' love is so intimate and blessed that He can bring utter bliss to His bride.
Jesus' love is so overflowing that He can overwhelm His bride with gifts.
Jesus' love is so attentive that He reacts to every wish and plea of His bride, and answers them—even when it does not seem so to us.
Jesus' love glows like a fire, so that it can set the bride's heart on fire again, if it has become indifferent, cold and lifeless.
Jesus' love is so radiant in its joy that it sheds its ray of joy upon the heart of the bride. It makes her happy and refreshes her when she is sad.
Jesus' love is so longsuffering that it never ceases to sustain the bride in all her sins

and difficulties, He will support her all the way.

Jesus' love is so rich that it can fulfill all the bride's longings for love.

Jesus' love is individual; He loves His bride as though He had only this one bride on earth and could not live without her.

Jesus' love is full of tender sympathy. There is nothing that the bride suffers without her Bridegroom's knowledge and without His suffering it with her.

Jesus' love is patient. It can wait until the bride's heart is ready and her love mature for all that He demands.

Jesus' love is forgiving. It veils the bride's sins and inadequacies so that they can no longer be seen.

Jesus' love is a generous love. He gives His all to His bride so that she partakes of His very being and all He has.

Jesus' love is a perfect love. It lacks neither fire nor gentleness, neither strength nor tenderness, neither holiness nor intimate affection.

Jesus' love is heavenly love. It contains the whole bliss of heaven. Here on earth He imparts this love to His bride.

Jesus' love is a holy love which draws His bride to live in the realm of His holiness.

Jesus' love is so pure that He can never disappoint anyone, let alone His bride.

Jesus' love is so tender and understanding that He can understand and refresh His bride with His love even in her smallest anxieties and emotions.[1]

BASILEA SCHLINK IN MY ALL FOR HIM

ENJOY HIS PRESENCE

Close your quiet time today by meditating on these words written by Charles Wesley:

Jesus, lover of my soul
Let me to Thy bosom fly,
While the nearer waters roll,
While the tempest still is high.
Hide me, O my Savior hide,
'Til the storm of life is past;
Safe into the haven guide,
O receive my soul at last!

Other refuge have I none,
Hangs my helpless soul on Thee;
Leave, O leave me not alone,
Still support and comfort me.
All my trust on Thee is stayed,
All my help from Thee I bring;

Cover my defenseless head
With the shadow of Thy wing.

Plenteous grace with Thee is found,
Grace to cover all my sin.
Let the healing streams abound,
Make and keep me pure within.
Thou of life the fountain art,
Freely let me take of Thee;
Spring Thou up within my heart,
Rise to all eternity. Amen.

REST IN HIS LOVE

"'I love You, O LORD, my strength.' The LORD is my rock and my fortress and my deliverer,
My God, my rock, in whom I take refuge; my shield and the horn of my salvation, my
stronghold" (Psalm 18:1-2).

entrusted with a stewardship

When Jesus then saw His mother, and the disciple whom He loved standing nearby,
He said to His mother, "Woman, behold, your son!"
JOHN 19:26

Prepare Your Heart

As you become a disciple loved by Jesus, He will entrust you with greater responsibility in His kingdom. This is called *stewardship*. A good steward takes care of that which is entrusted to him or her. As Jesus was hanging from the cross, He looked down, and John was the only male disciple who had not run away in grief and fear. The disciple whom Jesus loved was there in Jesus' darkest hour. Jesus then knew He could entrust one to John who was dear to Him—His mother. Jesus said to John, "Behold, your mother" (John 19:27).

Today you will look at what happened that day. It was a moment etched in time for all to see thousands of years later and to understand what happens in the intimate love of Christ. He entrusts a stewardship to those He loves. This stewardship from Christ includes many things: His Word containing His commands, instruction, and promises; His purposes; His people; His ministry. Those who know Christ's love are faithful in those things that He has entrusted to them.

Today, as you begin your quiet time, meditate on Psalm 65. Record your favorite part of this psalm.

READ AND STUDY GOD'S WORD

1. Turn to John 19:25-27. What happened in the final moments before Jesus said, "It is finished" (John 19:30)?

2. What does this act of Jesus tell you about what John meant to Him?

3. To love Jesus is always a prerequisite for being a good steward and servant. Read John 21:11-19. How does love relate to ministry and stewardship?

4. Look at the following passages about stewardship. What do you learn from each passage?
   1 Corinthians 4:1-2

   Galatians 2:7-8

   Ephesians 3:1-2

   Colossians 1:25

1 Peter 4:10

5. What can keep us from faithfully managing that which the Lord entrusts to us?

ADORE GOD IN PRAYER

Who do you resemble more: the disciples who ran from Jesus and the cross, or those who stayed near to Jesus in His darkest hour? Will you talk with the Lord about this today? Ask Him to give you that heart of love and devotion that keeps you near Him no matter what comes your way.

YIELD YOURSELF TO GOD

Sweet the moments, rich in blessing,
Which before the Cross I spend;
Life and health and peace possessing
From the sinner's dying Friend.

Truly blessed is this station,
Low before His Cross to lie;
While I see divine compassion
Beaming in His languid eye.

Love and grief my heart dividing,
With my tears His feet I'll bathe;
Constant still in faith abiding,
Life deriving from His death.

For Thy sorrows we adore Thee—
For the griefs that wrought our peace—
Gracious Savior! We implore Thee,
In our hearts Thy love increase.

WALTER SHIRLEY (1725–1786)

Enjoy His Presence

What has God entrusted to you? Do you see that your stewardship of those things is an indication of your love for the Lord? Love comes first. Stewardship and service follow. Focus on cultivating your intimacy with the Lord. How can you do that today? You will notice that serving your Lord and taking care of those things He has entrusted to you will be such a joy when you are cultivating your love for the Lord.

Rest in His Love

"As each one has received a special gift, employ it in serving one another as good stewards of the manifold grace of God" (1 Peter 4:10).

recognize Jesus at every turn

Therefore that disciple whom Jesus loved said to Peter, "It is the Lord."
JOHN 21:7

Prepare Your Heart

Even for those who are intimate with the Lord, there are times when He seems distant. The landscape of life darkens, perhaps because of feelings or circumstances, and disciples cannot seem to find their way. But those who love the Lord will keep going by the way they know, trusting in the Word of their Lord, even against all odds. And then, often when they least expect it, the Lord breaks through the clouds. Others do not notice, but those who know and love Christ know "it is the Lord." They recognize Him in action.

As you draw near to the Lord, meditate on the words of this prayer. Make them your own today.

> Oh Father of Jesus,
> Help me to approach thee with deepest reverence, not with presumption,
> Not with servile fear, but with holy boldness.
> Thou art beyond the grasp of my understanding,
> But not beyond that of my love,
> Thou knowest that I love thee supremely,
> For thou art supremely adorable, good, perfect.
> My heart melts at the love of Jesus,
> My brother, bone of my bone, flesh of my flesh,
> Married to me, dead for me, risen for me;
> He is mine and I am his,
> Given to me as well as for me;
> I am never so much mine as when I am his,

Or so much lost to myself until lost in him;
Then I find my true manhood.
But my love is frost and cold, ice and snow;
Let his love warm me,
Lighten my burden,
Be my heaven;
May it be more revealed to me in all its influences
That my love to him may be more fervent and glowing;
Let the mighty tide of his everlasting love
Cover the rocks of my sin and care;
Then let my spirit float above those things
Which had else wrecked my life.
Make me fruitful by living to that love,
My character becoming more beautiful every day.
If traces of Christ's love-artistry be upon me,
May he work on with his divine brush
Until the complete image be obtained
And I be made a perfect copy of him, my master.
O Lord Jesus, come to me,
O Divine Spirit, rest upon me,
O Holy Father, look on me in mercy for the sake of the well-beloved.[1]

FROM *THE VALLEY OF VISION*

READ AND STUDY GOD'S WORD

1. The "disciple whom Jesus loved" was part of some of the most crucial events involving Jesus. After His crucifixion and resurrection, Jesus surprised His disciples with His presence. Turn to John 21:1-7. What happened in this surprise visit by Jesus?

2. Read Luke 24. How did Jesus make Himself known to these various people? How did they respond? Record your insights.

3. What do you learn from the following verses about seeing and recognizing Jesus?
   1 Corinthians 13:12

   Ephesians 1:18-19

   Hebrews 11:1-2

   Hebrews 12:1-2,14

   1 John 3:2

4. How can you see and recognize Jesus?

ADORE GOD IN PRAYER

Think about the words of those people who came to Philip and said, "Sir, we wish to see Jesus" (John 12:21). Is that the desire of your heart today? Will you take some time now and write a prayer to the Lord in your Journal? Include in your prayer that which is most significant from your study in His Word today.

YIELD YOURSELF TO GOD

Believing, then, is directing the heart's attention to Jesus. It is lifting the mind to *behold the Lamb of God*, and never ceasing that beholding for the rest of our lives. At first this may be difficult, but it becomes easier as we look steadily at His wondrous Person, quietly and without strain. Distractions may hinder, but once the heart is committed to Him, after each brief excursion away from Him the attention will return again and rest upon Him like a wandering bird coming back to its window. . . . When we lift our inward eyes to gaze upon God we are sure to meet friendly eyes gazing back at us, for it is written that the eyes of the Lord run to and fro throughout all the earth. The sweet language of experience is *Thou God seest me*. When the eyes of the soul looking out meet the eyes of God looking in, heaven has begun right here on this earth. . . . Lift your heart and let it rest upon Jesus and you are instantly in a sanctuary though it be a Pullman berth or a factory or a kitchen. You can see God from anywhere if your mind is set to love and obey Him. . . . Long periods of Bible meditation will purify our gaze and direct it; church attendance will enlarge our outlook and increase our love for others. Service and work and activity; all are good and should be engaged in by every Christian. But at the bottom of all these things, giving meaning to them, will be the inward habit of beholding God. A new set of eyes (so to speak) will develop within us enabling us to be looking at God while our outward eyes are seeing the scenes of this passing world.[2]

A. W. TOZER IN THE PURSUIT OF GOD

Declarations of faith often seem untrue at first, so apparently real are the seen reasons for doubt and discouragement. But the unseen facts are truer than the seen, and if the faith that lays hold of them is steadfastly persisted in, they never fail in the end to prove themselves to be the very truth of God.

HANNAH WHITALL SMITH IN THE GOD OF ALL COMFORT

Taken aside by Jesus,
to feel the touch of His hand;
to rest for awhile in the shadow,
Of the rock in a weary land.

Taken aside by Jesus,
In the loneliness dark and drear,
Where no other comfort may reach me,
Than His voice to my heart so dear.
Taken aside by Jesus,
To be quite alone with Him,

To hear His wonderful tones of love
'Mid the silence and shadows dim.
Taken aside by Jesus,
Shall I shrink from the desert place;
When I hear as I never heard before,
And see Him face to face.[3]

MRS. CHARLES COWMAN IN *STREAMS IN THE DESERT*

See God in everything, and God will calm and color all that thou dost see. It may be that the circumstances of our sorrows will not be removed, their condition will remain unchanged; but if Christ, as Lord and Master of our life, is brought into our grief and gloom, *He will compass us about with songs of deliverance.* To see HIM, and to be sure that His wisdom cannot err, His power cannot fail, His love can never change; to know that even His direst dealings with us are for our deepest spiritual gain, is to be able to say, in the midst of bereavement, sorrow, pain, and loss, *The Lord gave, the Lord hath taken away; blessed be the name of the Lord.* Nothing else but *seeing God in everything* will make us loving and patient with those who annoy and trouble us. They will be to us then only instruments for accomplishing His tender and wise purposes toward us, and we shall even find ourselves at last inwardly thanking them for the blessings they bring us. Nothing else will completely put an end to all murmuring or rebelling thoughts.[4]

HANNAH WHITALL SMITH AS SHARED BY MRS. CHARLES COWMAN IN *STREAMS IN THE DESERT*

I saw HIM in the morning light,
He made the day shine clear and bright;
I saw HIM in the noontide hour,
And gained from HIM refreshing shower.
At eventide, when worn and sad,
HE gave me help, and made me glad,
At midnight, when on tossing bed
My weary soul to sleep HE led.

I saw HIM when great losses came,
And found HE loved me just the same.
When heavy loads I had to bear,
I found HE lightened every care.
By sickness, sorrow, sore distress,
HE calmed my mind and gave me rest,
HE'S filled my heart with gladsome praise
Since I gave HIM the upward gaze.[5]

A. E. FINN AS SHARED BY MRS. CHARLES COWMAN IN *STREAMS IN THE DESERT*

ENJOY HIS PRESENCE

Are you in the habit of recognizing Jesus at every turn in your life? Are your eyes trained to behold the Lord? Are you looking for Him, and is the gaze of your soul filled with Him? This is a great quality in the life of the one who knows and enjoys the love of Christ. As you think about what you have seen today in your quiet time, how can you learn to recognize Jesus at every turn? What will be the result when you recognize Jesus in your life?

REST IN HIS LOVE

"Were not our hearts burning within us while He was speaking to us on the road, while He was explaining the Scriptures to us?" (Luke 24:32).

proclaim the message of Christ

What we have seen and heard we proclaim to you also.
1 JOHN 1:3

Prepare Your Heart

Those who love Christ love to proclaim the message of Christ. His message drives them onward. They cannot help sharing what they have seen and heard. This was true of John, the disciple whom Jesus loved. Just prior to His ascension to heaven, Jesus said to His disciples, "You will receive power when the Holy Spirit has come upon you; and you shall be My witnesses both in Jerusalem, and in all Judea and Samaria, and even to the remotest parts of the earth" (Acts 1:8). And this is exactly what John did for the rest of his life. This is what every disciple of Jesus is filled with the desire to do: proclaim the message of Christ.

Reuben Archer Torrey was a genius of ministry, renowned as an educator, pastor, world evangelist, and author. He was a man of prayer and a student of the Bible. He proclaimed Christ at every opportunity. It is said that he daily read the Bible in four languages and had a good working knowledge of Greek and Hebrew. Some church historians believe Torrey did more to promote personal evangelism than any other one man since the days of the apostles.

Torrey grew up in a Christian home, read what it meant to be a Christian, but was skeptical of giving his life to Christ, because he was afraid he would have to become a preacher instead of a lawyer. He attended Yale University at the age of fifteen. One night, during an episode of tremendous fear, he knelt by his bed and asked the Lord to come into his heart. He told the Lord he would even be a preacher if that was what God wanted. He attended Yale Divinity School after his graduation from Yale University. He became obsessed with winning people to Christ.

While in seminary he heard D. L. Moody speak. Torrey and his friends were so amazed at Moody's preaching that they asked him to show them how to win others to Christ. Moody said, "Go at it! That's the best way to learn." So Torrey just began telling others about Christ, one by one. His favorite saying throughout his life was, "I love to preach the gospel of Jesus Christ." After seminary he pastored a church and superintended the Congregational City Mission Society. Then, at the age of thirty-three, Torrey became the first superintendent of what was to become Moody Bible Institute (MBI). It is thought that the success of MBI can probably be attributed to Torrey's contributions more than any other individual's.

When Moody died in 1899, it was Torrey who became his successor in world evangelism. Torrey began to have a burden to pray that God would send him around the world with the gospel. In the next few years, as he traveled throughout the world, he saw some 102,000 come to Christ. He also wrote at least forty books. His book *How to Promote and Conduct a Successful Revival* is considered one of the best on personal and mass evangelism ever written.

Torrey's life reminds us of that phrase once again: "The world has yet to see what God can do in and through the life of one whose heart is wholly yielded to Him." At Torrey's funeral, Will Houghton said this: "Those who knew Dr. Torrey more intimately knew him as a man of regular and uninterrupted prayer. He knew what it meant to pray without ceasing. With hours set systematically apart for prayer, he gave himself diligently to this ministry."[1]

It all comes down to this one thing: your whole life, who you are and how you live, flows out of your intimate relationship with Christ. It's wonderful to know that you are living a life of purpose and influencing hundreds, even thousands, with the message of Christ. You may not see the impact until you enter the portals of heaven. But you can know that your intimacy with God affects others.

READ AND STUDY GOD'S WORD

1. John could not help proclaiming the message of Christ. Turn to Acts 3:1–4:33. In these events, Peter and John have many opportunities to share the Lord's message with others. Write out every phrase or sentence in these two chapters that gives you insight into proclaiming the message of Christ.

2. John also wrote letters to proclaim the message. Read 1 John 1:1-5. What did John proclaim?

3. What is your most significant observation about sharing the message of Christ with others?

ADORE GOD IN PRAYER

Teach me to do the thing that pleaseth Thee;
Thou art my God, in Thee I live and move;
Oh, let Thy loving Spirit lead me forth
Into the land of righteousness and love.

Thy love the law and impulse of my soul,
Thy righteousness its fitness and its plea,
Thy loving Spirit mercy's sweet control
To make me liker, draw me nearer Thee.

My highest hope to be where, Lord, Thou art,
To lose myself in Thee my richest gain,
To do Thy will the habit of my heart,
To grieve the Spirit my severest pain.

Thy smile my sunshine, all my peace from thence,
From self alone what could that peace destroy?
Thy joy my sorrow at the least offence,
My sorrow that I am not more Thy joy.

JOHN S. B. MONSELL (1811–1875)

YIELD YOURSELF TO GOD

Get it thoroughly understood between yourself and God that He wants you to do this work, and that by His grace you are going to do it whatever it costs. This is one of the most important things in starting out to do open-air meetings. You are bound to make a failure unless you settle this at the start. Open-air work has its discouragements, its difficulties and its almost insurmountable obstacles, and unless you start out knowing that God has called you to the work, and come what will, you will go through with it, you are sure to give it up. . . . It is the man who is absolutely loyal to God's Word, and who is familiar with it and constantly uses it, who succeeds in the open air. God often takes a text that is quoted, and uses it for the salvation of some hearer. Arguments and illustrations are forgotten, but the text sticks and converts.[2]

R. A. TORREY IN "OPEN-AIR MEETINGS"

The day of golden opportunity is today. Golden opportunities, opportunities of price-less worth, are open to every one of us today. But *tomorrow* has no sure promise for any one of us. The Holy Spirit says *Today*, and Conscience also cries, *Today*, and the voice of Reason and the voice of History and the voice of Experience unite in one loud cho-rus and shout, *Today*. Only the voices of indifference and laziness and folly murmur, *Tomorrow*. The Holy Spirit is ever calling, *Today*. Men in their folly are forever saying, *Tomorrow*. . . . The only action that is intelligent and wise for anyone who has not already accepted Jesus Christ is to accept Him right here tonight. Resolutions to do the right thing and the wise thing at some indefinite time in the future are of no value whatever. God's time is now. The Holy Spirit says *Today*.

R. A. TORREY IN "THE DAY OF GOLDEN OPPORTUNITY"

There is nothing else that draws like the uplifted Christ. Movies may get a crowd of empty-headed and empty-hearted young men and maidens, and even middle-aged folks without brains or moral earnestness, for a time, but nothing really draws and holds the men and women who are worthwhile like Jesus Christ lifted up. Nineteen centuries of Christian history prove the drawing power of Jesus when He is properly presented to men. I have seen some wonderful verification of the assertion of our text as to the marvelous drawing power of the uplifted Christ. In London, for two continu-ous months, six afternoons and evenings each week, I saw the great Royal Albert Hall filled and even jammed, and sometimes as many turned away as got in, though it would seat 10,000 people by actual count and stand 2,000 more in the dome. On the open-ing night of these meetings a leading reporter of the city of London came to me before the service began and said, "You have taken this building for two consecutive months?" "Yes." "And you expect to fill it every day?" "Yes." "Why," he said, "no one has ever attempted to hold two weeks' consecutive meetings here of any kind. Gladstone him-self could not fill it for two weeks. And you really expect to fill it for two months?" I replied, "Come and see." He came and he saw. On the last night, when the place was jammed to its utmost capacity and thousands outside clamored for admission, he came to me again and I said, "Has it been filled?" He smiled and said, "It has." But what filled it? No show on earth could have filled it once a day for many consecutive days. The preacher was no remarkable orator. He had no gift of wit and humor, and would not have exercised it if he had. The newspapers constantly called attention to the fact that he was no orator, but the crowds came and came and came. On both rainy days, and fine days they crowded in or stood outside, oftentimes in a downpour of rain, in the vain hope of getting in. *What Drew Them?* The uplifted Christ preached and sung in the power of the Holy Spirit, given in answer to the daily prayers of 40,000 people scattered throughout the earth.

R. A. TORREY IN "THE GREAT ATTRACTION: THE UPLIFTED CHRIST"

ENJOY HIS PRESENCE

Close your time with the Lord today by thinking about these words written by Fanny Crosby. Imagine that this is the cry of hearts all around you, whose deepest desire is to know Jesus.

> Tell me the story of Jesus,
> Write on my heart every word.
> Tell me the story most precious,
> Sweetest that ever was heard.
> Tell how the angels in chorus,
> Sang as they welcomed His birth.
> "Glory to God in the highest!
> Peace and good tidings to earth."

> Refrain:

> Tell me the story of Jesus,
> Write on my heart every word.
> Tell me the story most precious,
> Sweetest that ever was heard.

> Fasting alone in the desert,
> Tell of the days that are past.
> How for our sins He was tempted,
> Yet was triumphant at last.
> Tell of the years of His labor,
> Tell of the sorrow He bore.
> He was despised and afflicted,
> Homeless, rejected and poor.

> Refrain

> Tell of the cross where they nailed Him,
> Writhing in anguish and pain.
> Tell of the grave where they laid Him,
> Tell how He liveth again.
> Love in that story so tender,
> Clearer than ever I see.

Stay, let me weep while you whisper,
Love paid the ransom for me.

Refrain

Will you tell others the best news that they could ever know? Will you proclaim what you have seen and heard about Jesus?

REST IN HIS LOVE
"But thanks be to God, who always leads us in triumph in Christ, and manifests through us the sweet aroma of the knowledge of Him in every place" (2 Corinthians 2:14).

catch a glimpse of His glory

Then I turned to see the voice that was speaking with me.
REVELATION 1:12

Prepare Your Heart

John, the disciple Jesus loved, was probably the only one of the apostles still living when he was exiled to Patmos because of his faithfulness to proclaim Christ. According to church tradition, primarily the writings of Irenaeus, he was the pastor of the church at Ephesus just before his exile. Remains of the churches at Ephesus actually bear John's name, corroborating the literary evidence.

What must it have been like to be the last living one who walked with Jesus?

John was exiled to a small, rocky island that was reserved for Roman political prisoners. There, in the darkness of his circumstances, in the middle of nowhere, he was given a glimpse of Christ's glory. It was a glimpse of the eternal, the ultimate consummation of an intimate relationship with the Lord Jesus Christ. The same can happen to you in your dark hour.

As you begin your quiet time, think about these words written by Fanny Crosby:

Breaking through the clouds that gather,
O'er the Christian's natal skies,
Distant beams, like floods of glory,
Fill the soul with glad surprise;
And we almost hear the echo
Of the pure and holy throng,
In the bright, the bright forever,
In the summer land of song.

Refrain:
On the banks beyond the river
We shall meet, no more to sever;

In the bright, the bright forever,
In the summer land of song.

Yet a little while we linger,
Ere we reach our journey's end;
Yet a little while of labor,
Ere the evening shades descend;
Then we'll lay us down to slumber,
But the night will soon be o'er;
In the bright, the bright forever,
We shall wake, to weep no more.

Refrain

O the bliss of life eternal!
O the long unbroken rest!
In the golden fields of pleasure,
In the region of the blest;
But, to see our dear Redeemer,
And before His throne to fall,
There to bear His gracious welcome,
Will be sweeter far than all.

Refrain

READ AND STUDY GOD'S WORD

1. John was given a glimpse of God's glory while exiled on Patmos. Read Revelation 1. What happened to John? What did he see?

2. The phrases "I saw" and "I heard" are repeated over and over in the book of Revelation. It must have been exciting to be the one who saw and heard these things. Read Revelation 19:7-16. What did John see? What did he learn about the future of the bride of Jesus Christ?

3. What did John see in Revelation 21:1-4?

4. What did John see in Revelation 22:1-5?

5. God has given us His Word. There we, even now, may catch a glimpse of His glory. We do see "in a mirror dimly" (1 Corinthians 13:12). That mirror is the Word of God (see James 1:22-25). With that in mind, read 1 Corinthians 2:9-16. What can you catch a glimpse of, and how?

ADORE GOD IN PRAYER

O let the great cloud of witnesses, who have gone before us and entered into their rest, be an example to me of a godly life. Even now may I be refreshed with their joy and run with patience the remainder of the race that is set before me.[1]

F. B. MEYER IN *DAILY PRAYERS*

YIELD YOURSELF TO GOD

The intimacy and closeness experienced during the engagement period is only the prelude to the much more joyous intimacy of married life. In many places, Scripture envisions the consummation of such a union between Christ and His chosen Bride. It is the event for which not only the believer but all heaven is waiting. It is the climax that the redeemed of every age have looked and longed for.[2]

J. OSWALD SANDERS IN *ENJOYING INTIMACY WITH GOD*

What must heaven keep in store for us, if earth can offer us such unimaginable beauty? I have a tiny blue feather, so unbelievably blue that you feel as you look at it that only God could have thought of such a blue. I wonder what heaven will have for us in the way of surprises of color. Did you ever think how impossible it is to imagine a new color, and yet the Creator of color is not confined to seven and combinations of seven. What dazzling mysteries lie just beyond our view! I do not wonder that men who were given glimpses of these glories fell back on similitudes and the phrase *as it were*. *As it were a paved work of sapphire stone, and as it were the body of heaven in all his clearness* (Exodus 24:10). But it will be Love that makes heaven. Beauty alone would leave us cold. Think what it will be to look around and not see a single unloving face, and to know that in all heaven there is not one who can think an unkind thought.[3]

AMY CARMICHAEL IN *FRAGMENTS THAT REMAIN*

ENJOY HIS PRESENCE

> There is a balm for every pain,
> a medicine for all sorrow;
> the eye turned backward to the Cross,
> and forward to the morrow.
> The morrow of the glory and the psalm,
> When He shall come;
> The morrow of the harping and the palm,
> The welcome home.
> Meantime in His beloved hands our ways,
> And on His Heart the wandering heart at rest;
> And comfort for the weary one who lays
> His head upon His Breast.

GERHARD TERSTEEGEN (1697–1769)

REST IN HIS LOVE

"But just as it is written, 'Things which eye has not seen and ear has not heard, and which have not entered the heart of man, all that God has prepared for those who love Him'" (1 Corinthians 2:9).

Dear Friend,

The next two days are your opportunity to spend time reviewing what you have learned this week. You may wish to write your thoughts and insights in your Journal. As you think about all you have learned about the life of John and what it means to be that disciple whom Jesus loves, write down:

Your most significant insight:

Your favorite quote:

Your favorite verse:

What will it take to be able to say that you are a disciple whom Jesus loves? Is that the desire of your heart?

As you think through all these quiet times on intimacy with the Lord, which week was your favorite, and why?

What is the most important truth you learned as you spent time with the Lord using *A Heart That Dances?*

Turn to the prayer you wrote at the beginning of your journey through these quiet times (page 18, in the Introduction). How has what you have learned made a difference in your relationship with the Lord?

Close this week by meditating on these words by Charles Spurgeon and then the prayer that follows:

Spiritual knowledge of Christ will be a personal knowledge. I cannot know Jesus through another person's acquaintance with Him. No, I must know Him myself; I must know Him on my own account. It will be an intelligent knowledge—I must know Him, not as the visionary dreams of Him, but as the Word reveals Him. I must know His natures, divine and human. I must know His offices—His attributes—His works—His shame—His glory. I must meditate upon Him until I *comprehend with all saints what is the breadth, and length, and depth, and height; and know the love of Christ, which passeth knowledge.* It will be an affectionate knowledge of Him; indeed, if I know Him at all, I must love Him. An ounce of heart knowledge is worth a ton of head learning. Our knowledge of Him will be a satisfying knowledge. When I know my Saviour, my mind will be full to the brim—I shall feel that I have that which my spirit panted after. *This is that bread whereof if a man eat he shall never hunger.* At the same time it will be an exciting knowledge; the more I know of my Beloved, the more I shall want to know. The higher I climb the loftier will be the summits which invite my eager footsteps. I shall want the more as I get the more. Like the miser's treasure, my gold will make me covet more. To conclude; this knowledge of Christ Jesus will be a most happy one; in fact, so elevating, that sometimes it will completely bear me up above all trials, and doubts, and sorrows; and it will, while I enjoy it, make me something more than *Man that is born of woman, who is of few days, and full of trouble;* for it will fling about me the immortality of the ever living Saviour, and gird me with the golden girdle of His eternal joy. Come, my soul, sit at Jesus' feet and learn of Him all this day.[1]

Lord we love to read Your poetry;
We love to read Your Word.
Through Your pen of life you have given us a picture
Of Your presence, Your love, Your mercy, and Your grace.
Through the life of Moses You showed us servant-hood, faithfulness and trust;
Through Joshua—a soldier fighting in your name; carrying out what Moses began,
Leading a people to the promised land.
Through the great prophets of old Your faithfulness and love of Your people were
    told.
Through David, Your chosen King—a man after Your own heart—who showed us
    reverence,
Leadership, obedience and respect for You Oh Lord—Poetry at its best;
David showed us You, my Lord and Your Glory.
Through Isaiah You showed knowledge and truth;
Through Hosea faithfulness and trust and love of a people.
These are just a few. So many spoke and wrote Your Word from the heart, face to
    face with You.
Lord, then You gave us Your greatest gift, Your Son,
And with Him You sent those to chronicle His life—Matthew, Mark, Luke, and
    John, my favorite, the disciple whom Jesus loved and who wrote of his
Savior's highest Accomplishments and of who He was:
"In the beginning was the Word, and the Word was with God,
And the Word was God. He was with God in the beginning." (John 1:1)
You gave us Peter who wrote of Your love after Jesus had made him humble.
You gave us Paul to exemplify Your Word, make it true and righteous with all
    mankind.
Then through all the ages of time You have sent us poets and writers,
Wesley, Chambers, Tozer, Carmichael, Meyers, Lucado, Graham—to mention a very
    few.
You have created in their minds a great love for You and the Son and Holy Spirit.
No man will ever lack for reading of Your greatness,
And of the Son who gave His all for us, forgiving us, dying for us, showing us life
    after death, And interceding for us at Your throne oh Lord.
These true episodes of life are laid bare for all to read—
A description of You, our Creator and what You want us to be.
Lord, You have brought each of us to this time and place,
Where we share Your joy of the lives You touched so long ago.
Through our quiet time studies we read the poems, sing the hymns, weep and give
    thanks
Through devotional reading—learn of Your desires—
Written by the poets and writers of Your world

Who brings all together Your attributes of a good Christian Life;
They show us the adventure You bring my King—
Now we are able to see, to feel, to touch, to hear, and to taste of Your greatness and
    joy of life;
They touch the spirit with so much love that I venture to say in this prayer
We will dance and sing with joy,
Read of Your love, Your presence, Your true and all powerful Heart.
And when the day is over we each will come away with You, our Beloved.
In the precious Name of Jesus, Your Son, we pray this day,
Amen.[2]

KAREN MOUNCE

now that you have completed these quiet times

You have spent eight weeks consistently drawing near to God in quiet time with Him. That time alone with Him does not need to come to an end. What is the next step? To continue your pursuit of God, you might consider other books of quiet times in this series: *Pilgrimage of the Heart: Satisfy Your Longing for Adventure with God* and *Revive My Heart!: Satisfy Your Thirst for Personal Spiritual Renewal.*

You might choose to meet with friends as you spend time with the Lord using these books of quiet times. Leader's guides, audiotapes, and videotapes are available to accompany each book of quiet times. Apply practical ideas on how to have a quiet time, including choosing a Bible reading plan, setting aside a time and a place, using devotional books, and recording your insights in a quiet time notebook or journal.

Quiet Time Ministries has many resources to encourage you in your quiet time with God, including the Quiet Time Notebook, *Enriching Your Quiet Time* magazine, audiotapes, and videotapes. These resources may be ordered online from Quiet Time Ministries at www.quiettime.org. You may also call Quiet Time Ministries to order or request a catalog.

For more information, you may call or write to

Quiet Time Ministries
P.O. Box 14007
Palm Desert, California 92255
(800) 925-6458, (760) 772-2357
E-mail: catherine@quiettime.org
www.quiettime.org.

Pour out your heart like water in the presence of the Lord.
LAMENTATIONS 2:19, NIV

Pour out your heart like water in the presence of the Lord.
LAMENTATIONS 2:19, NIV

Pour out your heart like water in the presence of the Lord.
LAMENTATIONS 2:19, NIV

Pour out your heart like water in the presence of the Lord.
LAMENTATIONS 2:19, NIV

Pour out your heart like water in the presence of the Lord.
LAMENTATIONS 2:19, NIV

Pour out your heart like water in the presence of the Lord.
LAMENTATIONS 2:19, NIV

Pour out your heart like water in the presence of the Lord.
LAMENTATIONS 2:19, NIV

Pour out your heart like water in the presence of the Lord.
LAMENTATIONS 2:19, NIV

Pour out your heart like water in the presence of the Lord.
LAMENTATIONS 2:19, NIV

Do not be anxious about anything, but in everything, by prayer and petition, with thanksgiving, present your requests to God. And the peace of God, which transcends all understanding, will guard your hearts and your minds in Christ Jesus.
PHILIPPIANS 4:6-7, NIV

PRAYER FOR _____

DATE:

SCRIPTURE:

REQUEST:

ANSWER:

PRAYER FOR _____

DATE:

SCRIPTURE:

REQUEST:

ANSWER:

Do not be anxious about anything, but in everything, by prayer and petition, with thanksgiving, present your requests to God. And the peace of God, which transcends all understanding, will guard your hearts and your minds in Christ Jesus.
PHILIPPIANS 4:6-7, NIV

PRAYER FOR _____

DATE:

SCRIPTURE:

REQUEST:

ANSWER:

PRAYER FOR _____

DATE:

SCRIPTURE:

REQUEST:

ANSWER:

Do not be anxious about anything, but in everything, by prayer and petition, with thanksgiving, present your requests to God. And the peace of God, which transcends all understanding, will guard your hearts and your minds in Christ Jesus.
PHILIPPIANS 4:6-7, NIV

PRAYER FOR _____

DATE:

SCRIPTURE:

REQUEST:

ANSWER:

PRAYER FOR _____

DATE:

SCRIPTURE:

REQUEST:

ANSWER:

Do not be anxious about anything, but in everything, by prayer and petition, with thanksgiving, present your requests to God. And the peace of God, which transcends all understanding, will guard your hearts and your minds in Christ Jesus.
PHILIPPIANS 4:6-7, NIV

PRAYER FOR _____

DATE:

SCRIPTURE:

REQUEST:

ANSWER:

PRAYER FOR _____

DATE:

SCRIPTURE:

REQUEST:

ANSWER:

Do not be anxious about anything, but in everything, by prayer and petition, with thanksgiving, present your requests to God. And the peace of God, which transcends all understanding, will guard your hearts and your minds in Christ Jesus.
PHILIPPIANS 4:6-7, NIV

PRAYER FOR _____

DATE:

SCRIPTURE:

REQUEST:

ANSWER:

PRAYER FOR _____

DATE:

SCRIPTURE:

REQUEST:

ANSWER:

Do not be anxious about anything, but in everything, by prayer and petition, with thanksgiving, present your requests to God. And the peace of God, which transcends all understanding, will guard your hearts and your minds in Christ Jesus.
PHILIPPIANS 4:6-7, NIV

PRAYER FOR _____

DATE:

SCRIPTURE:

REQUEST:

ANSWER:

PRAYER FOR _____

DATE:

SCRIPTURE:

REQUEST:

ANSWER:

Do not be anxious about anything, but in everything, by prayer and petition, with thanksgiving, present your requests to God. And the peace of God, which transcends all understanding, will guard your hearts and your minds in Christ Jesus.
PHILIPPIANS 4:6-7, NIV

PRAYER FOR _____

DATE:

SCRIPTURE:

REQUEST:

ANSWER:

PRAYER FOR _____

DATE:

SCRIPTURE:

REQUEST:

ANSWER:

Do not be anxious about anything, but in everything, by prayer and petition, with thanksgiving, present your requests to God. And the peace of God, which transcends all understanding, will guard your hearts and your minds in Christ Jesus.
PHILIPPIANS 4:6-7, NIV

PRAYER FOR _____

DATE:

SCRIPTURE:

REQUEST:

ANSWER:

PRAYER FOR _____

DATE:

SCRIPTURE:

REQUEST:

ANSWER:

Do not be anxious about anything, but in everything, by prayer and petition, with thanksgiving, present your requests to God. And the peace of God, which transcends all understanding, will guard your hearts and your minds in Christ Jesus.
PHILIPPIANS 4:6-7, NIV

PRAYER FOR _____

DATE:

SCRIPTURE:

REQUEST:

ANSWER:

PRAYER FOR _____

DATE:

SCRIPTURE:

REQUEST:

ANSWER:

Do not be anxious about anything, but in everything, by prayer and petition, with thanksgiving, present your requests to God. And the peace of God, which transcends all understanding, will guard your hearts and your minds in Christ Jesus.
PHILIPPIANS 4:6-7, NIV

PRAYER FOR _____

DATE:

SCRIPTURE:

REQUEST:

ANSWER:

PRAYER FOR _____

DATE:

SCRIPTURE:

REQUEST:

ANSWER:

notes

INTRODUCTION

1. From *The Pursuit of God* by A. W. Tozer © 1982, 1993 by Christian Publications, Inc. Reprinted by permission of the publisher. Page 17.
2. Used by permission of Quiet Time Ministries.

WEEK 1, DAY 1

1. *The Confessions of St. Augustine*, I, 1.
2. John Piper, *Desiring God* (Portland, Ore.: Multnomah, 1986), pp. 53-54.

WEEK 1, DAY 2

1. Used with permission from I PROMISE YOU A CROWN by David Hazard © 1995 Bethany House Publishers. All Rights Reserved. Page 45.

WEEK 1, DAY 3

1. From *The Pursuit of God* by A. W. Tozer © 1982, 1993 by Christian Publications, Inc. Reprinted by permission of the publisher. Page 78.
2. From *A 31-Day Experience: The Pursuit of God* by A. W. Tozer, compiled by Edythe Draper © 1995 by Christian Publications, Inc. Reprinted by permission of the publisher. Page 51.
3. Brother Lawrence, *The Practice of the Presence of God: The Best Rule of Holy Life.* For complete text, see www.ccel.org (search: Lawrence).
4. This material is taken from *My Utmost for His Highest* by Oswald Chambers. Copyright © 1935, by Dodd Mead & Co., renewed © 1963 by the Oswald Chambers Publications Assn. Ltd., and is used by permission of Discovery House Publishers, Box 3566, Grand Rapids, MI 49501. All rights reserved. From October 12.

WEEK 1, DAY 4

1. From *The Pursuit of God* by A. W. Tozer © 1982, 1993 by Christian Publications, Inc. Reprinted by permission of the publisher. Page 13.
2. Charles Spurgeon, *Morning and Evening* (Scotland: Christian Focus Publications, 1994), Jan. 28, evening.
3. Amy Carmichael, *Toward Jerusalem* (Fort Washington, Penn.: Christian Literature Crusade, 1936), p. 116. Reprinted by permission of the publisher.

WEEK 1, DAY 5

1. Arthur Bennett, ed., *The Valley of Vision* (Carlisle, Penn.: Banner Of Truth, 1994), Introduction. Used by permission.

2. From *The Pursuit of God* by A. W. Tozer © 1982, 1993 by Christian Publications, Inc. Reprinted by permission of the publisher. Pages 9-10.
3. John Piper, *The Pleasures of God* (Portland, Ore.: Multnomah, 1991), p. 189.
4. Amy Carmichael, *Toward Jerusalem* (Fort Washington, Penn.: Christian Literature Crusade, 1936), p. 10. Reprinted by permission of the publisher.

WEEK 1, DAYS 6–7
1. Hannah Whitall Smith, *The Christian's Secret of a Happy Life* (New York: Revell, 1941), pp. 223-224.

WEEK 2, DAY 1
1. Mrs. Charles Cowman, *Streams in the Desert* (Los Angeles: The Oriental Missionary Society, 1925), pp. 37-38.
2. Charles Spurgeon, *Spurgeon on Prayer and Spiritual Warfare* (New Kensington, Penn.: Whitaker House, 1998), pp. 329-330.
3. Amy Carmichael, *Gold by Moonlight* (Fort Washington, Penn.: Christian Literature Crusade, 1936), p. 155. Reprinted by permission of the publisher.

WEEK 2, DAY 3
1. Hannah Whitall Smith, *The Christian's Secret of a Happy Life* (New York: Revell, 1941), pp. 149-152.

WEEK 2, DAY 4
1. Arthur Bennett, ed., *The Valley of Vision* (Carlisle, Penn.: Banner Of Truth Trust, 1994), p. 160. Reprinted by permission of the publisher.
2. Amy Carmichael, *Whispers of His Power* (Fort Washington, Penn.: Christian Literature Crusade, 1982), pp. 20-21. Reprinted by permission of the publisher.
3. Mrs. Charles Cowman, *Streams in the Desert* (Los Angeles: The Oriental Missionary Society, 1925), p. 78.

WEEK 2, DAY 5
1. William T. Ellis, *Billy Sunday, The Man and His Message* (Philadelphia: L. T. Myers, 1914), pp. 155-156.

WEEK 2, DAYS 6–7
1. From Mrs. Charles Cowman, *Springs in the Valley* (Los Angeles: The Oriental Missionary Society, 1939), p. 4.

WEEK 3, DAY 1
1. Rosalind Rinker, *Prayer Conversing with God* (Grand Rapids, Mich.: Zondervan Publishing House, 1970), p. 19. Used by permission of the publisher.
2. This material is taken from p. 11 of *Enjoying Intimacy with God* by J. Oswald Sanders. Copyright © 2000. Used by permission of Discovery House Publishers, Box 3566, Grand Rapids, MI 49501. All rights reserved.

3. Copied from *The Transforming Power of Prayer: Deepening Your Friendship with God,* James Houston © 1996. Used by permission of NavPress (*www.navpress.com*). Page 5.
4. From *The Divine Conquest* by A. W. Tozer © 1950 by Christian Publications, Inc. Used by permission. Page 24.

WEEK 3, DAY 2

1. Reprinted from *Daily Prayers.* Copyright © 1995 by Harold Shaw Publishers. WaterBrook Press, Colorado Springs, CO. All rights reserved.
2. Charles Swindoll, *Moses* (Nashville, Tenn.: W Publishing Group, 1999), pp. 95, 97-98. Reprinted by permission of the publisher. All rights reserved.
3. From *Men Who Met God* by A. W. Tozer © 1986 by Christian Publications, Inc. Reprinted by permission of the publisher. Page 72.
4. From *The Divine Conquest* by A. W. Tozer © 1950 by Christian Publications, Inc. Reprinted by permission of the publisher. Page 27.

WEEK 3, DAY 3

1. Andrew Murray, *Humility* (Old Tappan, N.J.: Revell, n.d.), p. 9.
2. Frank E. Gaebelein, *Expositor's Bible Commentary: OT,* vol. 2 (Grand Rapids, Mich.: Zondervan Publishing House, 1990), pp. 315-316. Reprinted by permission of the publisher.
3. Murray, pp. 31-32.

WEEK 3, DAY 4

1. David J. Fant Jr., *A. W. Tozer: A Twentieth-Century Prophet* (Harrisburg, Penn.: Christian Publications, 1964), p. 41. Reprinted by permission of the publisher.
2. Warren Wiersbe, comp., *The Best of A. W. Tozer* (Harrisburg, Penn.: Christian Publications, 1978), p. 9. Reprinted by permission of the publisher.
3. Fant, pp. 18-19. Reprinted by permission of the publisher.
4. Amy Carmichael, *Toward Jerusalem* (Fort Washington, Penn.: Christian Literature Crusade, 1936), p. 115. Reprinted by permission of the publisher.
5. Andrew Murray, *The Inner Life* (Grand Rapids, Mich.: Zondervan Corporation, 1980), p. 17. Reprinted by permission of the publisher.
6. A. W. Tozer, *The Pursuit of God* (Camp Hill, Penn.: Christian Publications), p. 15. Reprinted by permission of the publisher.

WEEK 3, DAY 5

1. D. W. Lambert, *Oswald Chambers: An Unbribed Soul* (Fort Washington, Penn.: Christian Literature Crusade, 1968), p. 46. Reprinted by permission of the publisher.
2. Lambert, p. 70. Reprinted by permission of the publisher.
3. This material is taken from *My Utmost for His Highest* by Oswald Chambers. Copyright © 1935 by Dodd Mead & Co., renewed © 1963 by the Oswald Chambers Publications Assn. Ltd., and is used by permission of Discovery House Publishers, Box 3566, Grand Rapids, MI 49501. All rights reserved. From December 27 reading.
4. Taken from *The Divine Conquest* by A. W. Tozer © 1950 by Christian Publications, Inc. Reprinted by permission of the publisher. Page 22.

WEEK 3, DAYS 6–7

1. This material is taken from *Enjoying Intimacy with God* by J. Oswald Sanders. Copyright © 2000. Used by permission of Discovery House Publishers, Box 3566, Grand Rapids, MI 49501. All rights reserved. Page 17.
2. Mrs. Charles Cowman, *Streams in the Desert* (Los Angeles: The Oriental Missionary Society, 1925), p. 212.

WEEK 4, DAY 1

1. Reprinted from *Daily Prayers*. Copyright © 1995 by Harold Shaw Publishers. WaterBrook Press, Colorado Springs, CO. All rights reserved. Page 104.
2. Taken from *Jesus Man of Joy*. Copyright © 1999 by Sherwood E. Wirt. Published by Harvest House Publishers, Eugene, OR 97402. Used by permission. Pages 85-87.
3. Alan Redpath, *The Making of a Man of God* (Old Tappan, N.J.: Revell, a division of Baker, 1962), pp. 15-16. Reprinted by permission of the publisher.

WEEK 4, DAY 2

1. Andrew Murray, *The Inner Life* (Grand Rapids, Mich.: Zondervan Corporation, 1980), p. 74. Used by permission of the publisher.
2. Alan Redpath, *The Making of a Man of God* (Old Tappan, N.J.: Revell, a division of Baker Book House Company, 1962), pp. 158, 164. Reprinted by permission of the publisher.

WEEK 4, DAY 3

1. Taken from "Sketch of Samuel Rutherford" by Rev. Andrew Bonar in *The Letters of Samuel Rutherford* (1664, 1891. Reprint, Carlisle, Penn.: Banner Of Truth, 1984), p. 5.
2. *The Letters of Samuel Rutherford* (1664, 1891. Reprint, Carlisle, Penn.: Banner Of Truth, 1984), pp. 455-457.

WEEK 4, DAY 4

1. Alan Redpath, *The Making of a Man of God* (Old Tappan, N.J.: Revell, a division of Baker Book House Company, 1962), p. 54. Reprinted by permission of the publisher.
2. This material is taken from *My Utmost for His Highest* by Oswald Chambers. Copyright © by Dodd Mead & Co., renewed © 1963 by the Oswald Chambers Publications Assn. Ltd., and is used by permission of Discovery House Publishers, Box 3566, Grand Rapids, MI 49501. All rights reserved. From August 7.
3. Redpath, pp. 90, 93. Used by permission.

WEEK 4, DAY 5

1. Taken from *Jesus Man of Joy*. Copyright © 1999 by Sherwood E. Wirt. Published by Harvest House Publishers, Eugene, OR 97402. Used by permission. Page 95.
2. Shared by Brennan Manning at a youth conference. Used by permission of Brennan Manning.

WEEK 4, DAYS 6–7

1. A. W. Tozer, "Keys to the Deeper Life," *Sunday Magazine*, 1957, p. 34. Copyright © 1987 by Zondervan Publishing Corporation. Used by permission of the publisher.

WEEK 5, DAY 1

1. Mrs. Charles Cowman, *Streams in the Desert* (Los Angeles: The Oriental Missionary Society, 1925), pp. 200-201.
2. Amy Carmichael, *Thou Givest, They Gather* (Fort Washington, Penn.: Christian Literature Crusade, 1977), pp. 29-30. Reprinted by permission of the publisher.

WEEK 5, DAY 2

1. J. Robertson McQuilkin, *Understanding and Applying the Bible* (Chicago: Moody Press, 1983), p. 13. Reprinted by permission of the publisher.
2. *What the Bible Is All About* by Henrietta Mears. Copyright © 1953. Gospel Light/Regal Books, Ventura, CA 93003. Reprinted by permission of the publisher. Pages 20-21.
3. J. I. Packer, *Knowing God* (Downers Grove, Ill.: InterVarsity, 1973), p. 23.
4. Taken from *Galatians* by Merrill C. Tenney. Copyright © 1950 by Wm. B. Eerdmans Publishing Company, Grand Rapids, Mich. Reprinted by permission of the publisher. Pages 207-208.

WEEK 5, DAY 3

1. Leonard E. LeSourd, *The Best of Catherine Marshall* (Grand Rapids, Mich.: Chosen Books, a division of Baker Book House Company, 1993), p. 60. Reprinted by permission of the publisher.
2. LeSourd, pp. 60-61. Reprinted by permission of the publisher.
3. This material is taken from *My Utmost for His Highest* by Oswald Chambers. Copyright © 1935 by Dodd Mead & Co., renewed © 1963 by the Oswald Chambers Publications Assn. Ltd., and is used by permission of Discovery House Publishers, Box 3566, Grand Rapids, MI 49501. All rights reserved. From October 31.

WEEK 5, DAY 4

1. Corrie ten Boom, *Tramp for the Lord* (Grand Rapids, Mich.: Revell, a division of Baker Book House Company, 1974), p. 16. Reprinted by permission of the publisher.
2. Corrie ten Boom, *Each New Day* (Grand Rapids, Mich.: Revell, Spire Books, a division of Baker Book House Company, 1977), p. 71. Reprinted by permission of the publisher.
3. O. Hallesby, *Prayer* (Minneapolis, Minn.: Augsburg, 1931), pp. 44-47.
4. O. Hallesby, p. 26.
5. James H. McConkey, *Prayer* (Pittsburgh, Penn.: Silver Publishing Society, 1931), pp. 97-99.

WEEK 5, DAY 5

1. Reprinted from *Daily Prayers*. Copyright © 1995 by Harold Shaw Publishers. WaterBrook Press, Colorado Springs, CO. All rights reserved. Page 8.
2. Harold J. Ockenga, *The Comfort of God* (New York: Revell, a division of Baker Book House Company, 1944), pp. 132-134. Reprinted by permission of the publisher.
3. A. M. Overton, "Faith." Publisher unknown.

WEEK 5, DAYS 6–7

1. Donald Whitney, *Spiritual Disciplines for the Christian Life* (Colorado Springs, Colo.: NavPress, 1991), pp. 44, 46.

WEEK 6, DAY 1

1. From *The Pursuit of God* by A. W. Tozer © 1982, 1993 by Christian Publications, Inc. Reprinted by permission of the publisher. Page 20.
2. Robert Murray McCheyne, *Bethany* (Swengel, Penn.: Reiner Publications, 1974), pp. 5-6.
3. Henri Nouwen, *The Way of the Heart* (New York: Ballantine Books, 1981), p. 17.

WEEK 6, DAY 2

1. Amy Carmichael, *Toward Jerusalem* (Fort Washington, Penn.: Christian Literature Crusade, 1936). Reprinted by permission of the publisher. Page 70.
2. Taken from *God Tells the Man Who Cares* by A. W. Tozer © 1970 Christian Publications, Inc. Reprinted by permission of the publisher. Pages 17, 21.
3. S. D. Gordon, *Quiet Talks on Prayer* (New York: Grossett & Dunlap, by arrangement with Revell, 1904), pp. 163-164.
4. Gordon, pp. 165-168.

WEEK 6, DAY 3

1. Arthur Bennett, ed., *The Valley of Vision* (Carlisle, Penn.: Banner Of Truth, 1975), p. 184. Reprinted by permission of the publisher.

WEEK 6, DAY 4

1. Watchman Nee, *The Normal Christian Life* © 1957. Used by permission of Kingsway Publications, Lottbridge Drove, Eastbourne, England. Pages 274, 284.
2. Used with permission from *My All For Him* by Basilea Schlink © 1971 Bethany House Publishers. All Rights Reserved. Pages 97-101.
3. Charles Spurgeon, *Morning and Evening* (Scotland: Christian Focus Publications, 1994), Feb. 4, morning.
4. Written by Conni Hudson, leader of the original pilots of *Pilgrimage of the Heart; Revive My Heart O Lord;* and *A Heart That Dances,* during the pilot of this week of study, 2001. Used by permission of Conni Hudson.

WEEK 6, DAY 5

1. F. B. Meyer, *The Way into the Holiest* (Grand Rapids, Mich.: Baker, 1951), pp. 201-202.
2. Miles J. Stanford, *The Green Letters.* Copyright © 1975 by Miles J. Stanford. Used by permission of Zondervan. Page 12.
3. Charles Spurgeon, *Morning and Evening* (Scotland: Christian Focus Publications, 1994), Feb. 21, morning.

WEEK 6, DAYS 6–7

1. Robert Murray McCheyne, *Bethany* (Swengel, Penn.: Reiner Publications, 1974), chapt. 1.

WEEK 7, DAY 1

1. F. F. Bruce, *Paul: Apostle of the Heart Set Free* (Grand Rapids, Mich.: Wm. B. Eerdmans Publishing Company, 1977). Reprinted by permission of the publisher.

2. Rev. W. J. Conybeare and Rev. J. S. Howson, *The Life and Epistles of St. Paul* (Grand Rapids, Mich.: Wm. B. Eerdmans Publishing Company, 1978), p. 80. Reprinted by permission of the publisher.

3. Mrs. Charles Cowman, *Streams in the Desert* (Los Angeles: The Oriental Missionary Society, 1925), p. 146.

4. From *F. B. Meyer Devotional Commentary* © 1989 Tyndale House Publishers, Inc. Used by permission. All rights reserved. Page 541.

5. This material is taken from *My Utmost for His Highest* by Oswald Chambers. Copyright © 1935 by Dodd Mead & Co., renewed © 1963 by the Oswald Chambers Publications Assn. Ltd., and is used by permission of Discovery House Publishers, Box 3566, Grand Rapids, MI 49501. All rights reserved. From October 2.

6. Miles Stanford, *Principles of Spiritual Growth*, p. 11; used by permission of Back to the Bible, Lincoln, Nebraska.

7. This material is taken from *My Utmost for His Highest* by Oswald Chambers. Copyright © 1935 by Dodd Mead & Co., renewed © 1963 by the Oswald Chambers Publications Assn. Ltd., and is used by permission of Discovery House Publishers, Box 3566, Grand Rapids, MI 49501. All rights reserved. From October 11.

8. This material is taken from *Enjoying Intimacy with God* by J. Oswald Sanders. Copyright © 2000. Used by permission of Discovery House Publishers, Box 3566, Grand Rapids, MI 49501. All rights reserved. Page 109.

WEEK 7, DAY 2

1. From A. W. Tozer, *The Christian Book of Mystical Verse* (Camp Hill, Penn.: Christian Publications, 1963), p. 106-107. Reprinted by permission of the publisher.

2. D. L Moody, *Moody's Latest Sermons* (New York: Revell, 1900), pp. 39-41.

3. Mrs. Charles Cowman, *Streams in the Desert* (Los Angeles: The Oriental Missionary Society, 1925), p. 157.

WEEK 7, DAY 3

1. F. B. Meyer, *Great Men of the Bible*, vol. 2 (Grand Rapids, Mich: Zondervan Corporation, 1982), pp. 331-332. Reprinted by permission of the publisher.

WEEK 7, DAY 4

1. Reprinted from *Daily Prayers*. Copyright © 1995 by Harold Shaw Publishers. WaterBrook Press, Colorado Springs, CO. All rights reserved. Page 27.

2. F. F. Bruce, *Paul: Apostle of the Heart Set Free* (Grand Rapids, Mich: Wm. B. Eerdmans Publishing Company, 1977), pp. 181, 187. Reprinted by permission of the publisher.

3. Roger C. Palms, *Enjoying the Closeness of God* (Minneapolis, Minn.: Wide Publications, a ministry of the Billy Graham Evangelistic Association, 1989), pp. 131-132. Used by permission of Mr. Roger C. Palms.

4. Charles Spurgeon, *Morning and Evening* (Scotland: Christian Focus Publications, 1994), Dec. 27, evening.

Week 7, Day 5

1. This material is taken from *My Utmost for His Highest* by Oswald Chambers. Copyright © 1935 by Dodd Mead & Co., renewed © 1963 by the Oswald Chambers Publications Assn. Ltd., and is used by permission of Discovery House Publishers, Box 3566, Grand Rapids, MI 49501. All rights reserved. From January 24.
2. Taken from *The Set of the Sail* by A. W. Tozer © 1986 by Christian Publications, Inc. Reprinted by permission of the publisher. Pages 11-13.
3. Ella Wheeler Wilcox, "The Wind of Fate," in *World Voices* (New York: Hearst's International Library Company, 1916), p.51.

Week 7, Days 6–7

1. F. F. Bruce, *Paul: Apostle of the Heart Set Free* (Grand Rapids, Mich.: Wm. B. Eerdmans Publishing Company, 1977), pp. 459-460. Used by permission.
2. Charles Spurgeon, *Morning and Evening* (Scotland: Christian Focus Publications, 1994). Sept. 18, evening.

Week 8, Day 1

1. Used with permission from *My All For Him* by Basilea Schlink © 1971 Bethany House Publishers. All Rights Reserved. Pages 104-105.

Week 8, Day 3

1. Arthur Bennett, ed., *The Valley of Vision* (Carlisle, Penn.: Banner Of Truth, 1975), p. 25. Reprinted by permission of the publisher.
2. From *The Pursuit of God* by A. W. Tozer © 1982, 1993 by Christian Publications, Inc. Reprinted by permission of the publisher. Pages 90-96.
3. Mrs. Charles Cowman, *Streams in the Desert* (Los Angeles: The Oriental Missionary Society, 1925), p. 253.
4. From Cowman, pp. 271-272.
5. From Cowman, p. 272.

Week 8, Day 4

1. Will Houghton, *Moody Monthly*, Oct. 1936, p. 57.
2. R. A. Torrey, "Open-Air Meetings" in *How to Work for Christ* (Westwood, N.J.: Revell, n.d.), pp. 222-233.

Week 8, Day 5

1. Reprinted from *Daily Prayers*. Copyright © 1995 by Harold Shaw Publishers. WaterBrook Press, Colorado Springs, CO. All rights reserved. Page 87.
2. This material is taken from *Enjoying Intimacy with God* by J. Oswald Sanders. Copyright © 2000. Used by permission of Discovery House Publishers, Box 3566, Grand Rapids, MI 49501. All rights reserved. Page 145.
3. Amy Carmichael, *Fragments That Remain* © 1987 Christian Literature Crusade. Used by permission. Pages 150-151.

WEEK 8, DAYS 6–7

1. Charles Spurgeon, *Morning and Evening* (Scotland: Christian Focus Publications, 1994), Oct. 14, morning.

2. "A Thankful Prayer for God's Poets And Writers" by Karen Mounce. Written during the pilot of *A Heart That Dances*, August 2001. Used by permission of Karen Mounce.

about the author

CATHERINE MARTIN is a summa cum laude graduate of Bethel Theological Seminary with a Master of Arts in Theological Studies. She is founder and president of Quiet Time Ministries, director of Women's Ministries at Southwest Community Church, on the adjunct faculty of Biola University, and is dedicated to teaching devotion to God and His Word. Teaching at retreats and conferences, she challenges others to seek God and love Him with all their heart, soul, mind, and strength.

LOOK FOR THESE OTHER TITLES IN THE QUIET TIMES FOR THE HEART SERIES.

Pilgrimage of the Heart

Do you want to contemplate the fathomless, taste the infinite,
and delight in God's love? This devotional takes you through
the Psalms to a deeper understanding of God's greatness.

Revive My Heart!

Studying passages such as Psalm 119, this book looks at many aspects
of personal spiritual revival. Through this you can gain spiritual depth,
joy, and access to your heavenly Father's resources in times of trouble.

To get your copies, visit your local bookstore, call 1-800-366-7788,
or log on to www.navpress.com. Ask for a FREE catalog
of NavPress products. Offer #BPA.